Maman's Homesick Pie

Maman's Homesick Pie

A PERSIAN HEART IN AN AMERICAN KITCHEN

Donia Bijan

ALGONQUIN BOOKS OF CHAPEL HILL 2011

Published by
Algonquin Books of Chapel Hill
Post Office Box 2225
Chapel Hill, North Carolina 27515-2225

a division of
Workman Publishing
225 Varick Street
New York, New York 10014

Published simultaneously in Canada by Thomas Allen & Son Limited.
Design by Anne Winslow.

Library of Congress Cataloging-in-Publication Data
Bijan, Donia.
Maman's homesick pie : a Persian heart in an American kitchen /
by Donia Bijan.
p. cm.
ISBN 978-1-56512-957-3 (hardback)
1. Cooking, Iranian.   2. Cooking — California — San Francisco.
I. Bijan, Donia.   II. Title.
TX725.I7B55 2011
641.5955 — dc23   2011023858

10 9 8 7 6 5 4 3 2 1
First Edition

In memory of Atefeh and Bijan

For Luca

Contents

· ·

Author's Note

· ·

I WROTE THIS BOOK in an attempt to find answers to the questions I never asked my parents, such as *How did it feel to start your life from nothing?* as well as to give their grandchildren a context so that when we speak of Iran, they will see their connection to the elusive home of their parents and grandparents. And because I am a cook, not a reporter, I have told the story as I remember it, through the prism of food, changing the names of the characters to preserve their privacy, but holding their place at my table.

Maman's Homesick Pie

Introduction

··

MY MOTHER HAD been dead eight days when I showed up in her kitchen. There I was, on a gray January afternoon, with empty boxes and grocery bags, determined to cope with my colossal loss by salvaging a head of lettuce, a quart of milk, a pint of plain yogurt, and jar after jar of homemade pickled vegetables.

Walking down the hallway to her front door, I was no longer greeted by the familiar aroma of sweet Persian spices, nor could I hear the faint notes of the classical music station my mother tuned in to from morning until the evening news. I half expected her to open the door and pull me to her chest—*Here you are, darling, here you are*—and tell me it had been a huge mistake, that she had not been crushed under the wheels of the old lady's Mercedes coupe, that she had not been in that zippered orange body bag on the side of the road, that the mangled body we buried just a few days ago was not her. *Not her.*

But on that day and thereafter, no tender heart awaited me, no one strung endearments like garlands around me, and no one cared if I was tired or chilly or asked me if I needed a sweater. My mother's home smelled of tea and roses, but no kettle whistled, promising a steaming cup, served on a tray with a pitcher of milk and butter cookies on a linen doily.

For days it was quiet, methodical work—sorting and packing the boxes I had lined up by her cabinets like little coffins, filling them with cups and saucers wrapped in newspaper, and spoons, spatulas, and whisks. I labeled them in angry print with a thick black felt-tip marker, bound for a basement until the day a grandchild might hoist it up to her first home and delight in things her grandparents once used.

My mother's best china and silver were not in these boxes— they'd been looted from her home in Iran thirty years earlier. In the aftermath of a revolution that had targeted my parents as infidels and royalists, they had escaped a regime that would have paraded their slain bodies through the streets of Tehran. These boxes held the everyday household things that my parents had slowly accumulated since their exile. Which was more valuable—the heirloom silver or these mismatched cups from Goodwill? My mother had worked harder to buy this single Wedgwood cup.

I was not prepared for this sort of packing. My mother always helped *me* pack, for trips, slumber parties, and camp.

Packing for good like this, packing after someone dies, holds no promise. I had to wonder: Who would want this cardigan with her elbow impressions, or the scarf that had cradled her head, or her cream and white sling-back shoes? Who would sit in her knitting chair and finish that unfinished sweater from a pattern she had cut out of *Vogue,* rolled up neatly around her knitting needles? And so, my task soon became a battle between us. I chided her for having too many things—*Why must you have so many juice glasses?*—then scolded myself for being too keen on giving everything away to spare myself having to scrutinize it. At times I was downright careless, tossing into the giveaway box a rotating caddy of poker chips that my son, then two, loved to dump on the floor and stack back in place with chubby fingers, spending as long as it took. When my mother looked after him, I would come to fetch him and find the two of them on the floor, spinning the caddy and shrieking out the colors of the chips: *Red! Blue! Green!* If I kept it, he would ask for her. No. Let somebody else stumble upon this treasure on the dusty back shelves of a secondhand store. In rare moments of clarity, I went home with a random tea strainer or a cracked wooden spoon tucked into my coat pocket. I suppose I thought she had held these things long enough, and often enough, that they were no longer inanimate.

One afternoon I pulled open a kitchen drawer, expecting to find more spoons that I had missed. Instead I found it filled with papers, which I feared were receipts and warranty cards.

I was ready to nag her again, when I realized they were recipes, mostly handwritten, some cut out of newspapers, piled in no particular order.

On the floor, with the drawer on my lap, I tallied recipe after recipe of American dishes that she had made great efforts to master: coleslaw, banana bread, carrot cake, macaroni and cheese. There were recipes for chow mein with the prerequisite can of water chestnuts, microwave sweet-and-sour shrimp, and casseroles involving Campbell's cream of mushroom soup, many bearing the name of the friend, neighbor, or colleague who had given her the instructions, like "Peggy's Lemon Bars." There were also newspaper clippings dating from the fall of 1980—the year my parents had arrived in America and settled in Fresno—dedicated exclusively to holiday cooking: Christmas goose, chestnut stuffing, eggnog pound cake, and "party favorites" like cheesy stuffed mushrooms. Thumbing through her eclectic compilation, I knew I had stumbled upon something far more revealing than an avid cook's recipe file or even a box of old letters. In my lap, I held her story.

Why had a woman so well versed in Persian cuisine, who had weathered a revolution, exile, and threats to her life and had built her family a new home through sheer will, felt pushed to the other side of belonging? Not one to be left out, she had seen a vital connection between food and belonging. The Thanksgiving holiday was her initiation, as it had been for so many generations of immigrants, giving thanks for

an opportunity to begin again without the threat of perse-
cution. Though confronted with tastes, textures, and ingredients that eluded her, my mother learned to roast a turkey,
make giblet gravy, create a signature stuffing, bake yams and
sweet potatoes with brown sugar and butter, and line up jars
of cranberry sauce with orange peel to give to neighbors.

She liked to tell us the story of her first Thanksgiving,
when, alone with my father, she had made cheeseburgers for
dinner. She loved a good, juicy burger, shaping and seasoning
the patties with salt and pepper, browning them to medium
rare in her cast-iron skillet, toasting sesame buns, and tucking
pickles and hearts of butter lettuce drizzled with vinaigrette
inside. Just as my parents sat down to eat, they got a call from
a woman conducting a survey asking whether they were having a turkey. *Why, no! We're having cheeseburgers.* The caller
had expressed pity and suggested churches where meals were
served. *Humph!* My mother hung up, offended that this
stranger had called her house and assumed she couldn't afford
a turkey. From then on, she embraced Thanksgiving with Pilgrim resourcefulness, talking to the butcher early in Novem-
ber to reserve the best-looking bird, storing fresh cranberries
and pecans in the shell in case they became scarce in the days
before the holiday, reveling in the preparations for a feast.
Year after year, she exclaimed, *This is my favorite holiday!*

My mother had many stories, funny ones that made you
laugh out loud no matter how many times you heard them.
Most of the stories were told around the kitchen table, over

long family meals. My father, shoulders quivering, eyes tearing, always struggled to deliver a punch line, though we knew the endings and had already spiraled into giggles. But the story of exile is rarely funny. Sure, it has its hilarious moments, like the time my father looked out into the yard of his tidy suburban home and saw a mother raccoon staring back at him—*What is this beast? Whom do I call to come capture it?*—but it's not a story to tell around the table; it doesn't have a tidy beginning, middle, and end.

Exile is threaded into your daily life long after you have become a citizen and pledged your allegiance and can make the best brownies in the neighborhood. I was compelled to make sense of my parents' journey from Iran to America to understand the world they inhabited. Just five years shy of my mother's age when she immigrated, I have to wonder if I possess a fraction of her will to start over at square one. Now that her tablecloth has been folded for the last time, the recipes are my only key to unlocking my parents' experience as immigrants, looking back to see into their lives as I move forward into mine. It turns out, I don't need to forget to move on.

Persian Cardamom Tea

In most Iranian homes, there is no better way to begin a story than with a cup of tea, served hot, in a glass to better see its amber hue, with two lumps of sugar, and a dish of sweets.

To make a pot of Persian cardamom tea, first bring the kettle to a boil. Swirl some boiling water in your teapot to warm it and pour the water back into your kettle. Measure 2 heaping teaspoons of Darjeeling or Earl Grey tea leaves and 1 crushed cardamom pod and place in pot. Fill the teapot ¾ full with boiling water and allow the tea to steep for 10 minutes under a tea cozy. Pour a glass of tea, then empty it back into your teapot, both to make sure the color is even and to warm your glass.

To serve, fill each glass with tea, leaving room to add boiling water from the kettle for guests who prefer their tea weaker. Replace the teapot on the samovar or under the tea cozy to keep it hot. My mother learned to knit tea cozies when she was a student in England—colorful ones with big pom-poms.

The quality of the tea will change if steeped for too long, so offer refills quickly!

Orange Cardamom Cookies

Makes 3 dozen

8 ounces (2 sticks) unsalted butter
½ cup granulated sugar
1 egg yolk
Grated zest of 2 oranges
2 cups flour
½ teaspoon salt
½ teaspoon ground cardamom
1 tablespoon poppy seeds

1. Beat the butter in the bowl of an electric mixer until it whitens, about 2 minutes. Add the sugar and blend well. Add the egg yolk and orange zest. Scrape down the sides of the bowl. Combine the flour, salt, cardamom, and poppy seeds and fold in, mixing just enough to combine the dough. Form the dough into 2 logs, wrap in parchment paper, and chill for 30 minutes.

2. Preheat the oven to 350°F.

3. Using a sharp knife, slice the logs into ½-inch-thick rounds and place 1 inch apart on a nonstick or parchment-paper-lined cookie sheet. Bake approximately 12 to 15 minutes, until slightly golden around the edges.

Note: This dough keeps well in the freezer for 2 to 3 weeks.

Chapter 1

THE TEHRAN OF my childhood was cosmopolitan and multicultural, bearing little resemblance to our Western notion of contemporary Iran—that of a fearful nation beneath the glare of clerics and Revolutionary Guards. I was born in a hospital built brick by brick by my father. Fresh out of medical school, he combined a loan with all of his savings to buy land in undeveloped Tehran and open his own hospital. He was a sought-after obstetrician and knew that if he built the hospital, the patients would come. And they did. At all hours of the night, frantic husbands would pound on the iron gate while their pregnant wives howled in the darkness, waiting for *Doktor* to rush out in his robe and slippers to let them in.

My mother, a registered nurse and midwife schooled in England, had returned home to Tehran in 1952. Some years earlier, in 1945, just as the war ended, my grandparents had sent their eighteen-year-old daughter to England. She flew to London from a one-room airport speaking only two words of English: *good* and *hello*. My grandfather had arranged for an escort to meet her upon her arrival. My mother thought the taxi driver who held the car door open and greeted her, *Hello, love, need a lift?* was her escort. She got the *hello* part and hopped in the back, expecting him to know where to go. He didn't, so she directed him: *Good hotel!* The cabby wasn't taking any chances, so he dropped her off at the Grosvenor House.

My mother could not tell this story without throwing her head back to laugh out loud. In her first twenty-four hours away from home, Britain welcomed her in pomp and glory. Imagine her awe when the bellboy opened the door to a room with gilded mirrors and dark wood paneling, the downy duvet and tasseled cushions, the bathtub with gold fixtures. After studying a room-service menu on the bedside table, she pointed to the ice cream from the pictured items. And here she would stop to lick her lips before continuing her story:

My dears, I opened the door to find a young man in a tuxedo and white gloves holding a silver tray upon which sat a tall crystal goblet with three perfect balls of vanilla ice cream, and a ladyfinger perched on top. He said, Good evening, ma'am. *I said,* Hello. *He marched inside, snapped open a starched white place mat, set my ice cream down with a small glass of water, a napkin, and a tall spoon. Then he turned and asked me if I cared for breakfast the next morning. I said,* Good. *He bowed and left. Oh, that was the best ice cream I've ever had!*

The next morning, there was a knock on the door, and a silver trolley was wheeled in. Apparently the war had not depleted the Grosvenor House of their supply of eggs, sausages, butter, toast, and marmalade. Bewildered, she lifted up the silver domes one by one and ate her first English breakfast. *Good!*

After checking with every hotel in London, her escort tracked her down. She got the call from the desk and was soon counting out a stack of pounds from an envelope her father had carefully pinned inside her coat pocket. After that day, there wouldn't be any more ice cream and marmalade. The boardinghouse where she was to stay at her nursing school rationed their staples; sugar, butter, and eggs were luxuries.

What my mother left out of her stories from this period in her life was the homesickness she must have carried around like a stone in her stomach. After growing up with the affection and endearments that my grandmother wove even into her reproaches, my mother was now met with the stiff upper lip of her British matron overseer. For the first six months, my mother struggled with English, memorizing her nursing textbooks without understanding a word. Matron would rap her knuckles on the door when she saw the band of light in the dim dormitory hallway: *Lights out!* My mother learned to place a rolled-up towel under the door and read by candle-light. Once a week, she watched her classmates wash their hair in the sink. She had never done this, being used to baths, her mother scrubbing her back and combing out the tangled curls. When Matron gave her a bottle of shampoo, she had no idea what it was—she had always washed her hair with big cakes of soap. So she learned to fill the sink with water that ran cold and shampoo her hair—a task made far more difficult by her thick locks, which never quite dried in the damp air.

Slowly the memorized texts, Matron's commands, and the chatter by the fire in the common room began to make sense. She started stringing words together to make sentences, and English found a way into her speech. And in the meantime she mastered sink baths, learned to make her sugar and tea ration last through the week, figured out how to start a proper fire, and began to knit hats and tea cozies.

The girl from Iran was a quick study. She may not have known it then, but she was predisposed to the British brand of feminism, self-reliant and matter-of-fact, which had taken root in her. In Iran, despite her father's mild protest, she had walked every morning to tennis courts and swimming pools miles from her home. Not wanting the whole town gossiping about his daughter alone in the streets, he required that she be accompanied by one of her brothers. To this day, my uncle complains about how she used to shake him out of sleep at five thirty and stick a toothbrush in his mouth: *Wake up! Wake up! Brush your teeth! Wash your face! I'm going to be late!* She dragged him half-asleep and whimpering through dark streets for the hour-and-a-half walk across town, cutting off his slightest whine with, *Nonsense! A bit of fresh air and a brisk walk never killed anyone!*

Once she could speak the language, she didn't hesitate to find ways to do what she wanted to do in England, like learning to drive and acquiring her driver's license, and cycling all over Europe on her school holidays, oblivious to the fleets of men who followed her. She boasted of one suitor who inquired about her favorite flower, then went to Holland to bring her a small, exquisite bouquet of lily of the valley. She dismissed him simply as *daft*. On a very tight budget, she managed to satisfy her passion for classical music by skipping meals to attend concerts, swaying in the standing room. I doubt she would have sat down even if she'd had orchestra seats. Years later, at the symphony in Tehran, I watched her perched on the very edge of her seat while my father's chin sunk further into his chest. *How can you possibly sleep through Beethoven?* she chided him.

As a child I used to stare at the black-and-white photos from her years in England: A slim girl in a fitted white nurse's smock, a dark wool cape clasped with a metal brooch at the base of her long neck, and dark curls tucked beneath a white cap. Resting her hands on the bicycle handlebars, she is beaming. In other photos with classmates, turning to the camera, she is the only one smiling, compensating for the joylessness of the others. She would never squander this abundance of liberty.

She returned home seven years later, a stunning woman

who spoke the Queen's English, listened to classical music turned up very loud on her little hi-fi, smoked Winston cigarettes, kept a bust of Beethoven on her dresser, and carried a British driver's license in her purse. Soon after her return, she was working in a university hospital when she ran into my father in the elevator. He stood behind her, inches away from the slender curve of her shoulders, her dark hair gathered in a braided bun under her crisp nursing cap. My father was smitten. My mother soon charmed him with her no-nonsense disposition, her rapid one-two step down the hospital corridors, and her cool indifference to men. Within days he was knocking on my grandfather's door, asking for her hand.

The usual custom in Iran requires a suitor to send his parents to make a formal request for marriage, *khastegari*. My father, however, was never one to abide by custom. He considered himself independent of convention. Besides, if he had confided in his family and friends that he planned to ask for my mother's hand, they would have mocked his rash judgment and discouraged him from pursuing a girl from a family so far out of his league. But my grandfather, wary of another suitor he did not approve of, hovering in the wings, received my father kindly. He was invited to dinner and encouraged to bring his family elders.

Not wanting his family to speak on his behalf, since his father had passed away and his mother lived in northern Iran, he arrived without elders, dapper in a gray tailor-made suit and polished black patent leather shoes, a white satin handkerchief in his breast pocket. His trim mustache and sparkling blue eyes under the awning of thick eyebrows gave the impression of amusement. He charmed my grandmother, who was warm and lovely and an excellent cook. She, in turn, prepared a feast, as she often did for guests, and made one of his favorite dishes, *mirza ghasemi,* a rich eggplant appetizer she served with yogurt and fresh herbs. My grandparents welcomed his confidence, and my mother's youngest brother quickly fell under his spell, leaving only my mother's heart to conquer.

My mother found him terribly handsome with his bright blue eyes, uncommon for an Iranian, and she admired his mad independence from custom. She had grown impatient with her childhood sweetheart, who was afraid of her father and had postponed a proposal indefinitely. My father's persistence, and the courageous plans he had drawn up for their future to work as a team, disarmed her. I imagine he conjured images of precocious sons with blue eyes, a hospital where they would live and work side by side, and a garden with mulberry trees for his children to climb. Not long after the dinner with my grandparents, he called one afternoon to get her final answer to his proposal. My mother hesitated a moment too long and he took her silence as a yes. Within minutes, the doorbell rang and a young boy he had dispatched carried in a magnificent bouquet of white lilies and roses so large that his knees buckled under its weight. Years later, whenever my mother and father argued, she would always remind him that she had never actually said yes. My grandparents made elaborate wedding plans, booking the Officers' Club, ordering a seven-tiered wedding cake, buying new suits for my uncles. While the guest list soared to over a thousand, my mother found herself caught in a whirlwind with very little say. So when she went for the final fitting of her wedding dress, she insisted on just one thing, to wear her nursing cap under her veil.

By the time the hospital was built in 1960, my parents were teamed up, working feverishly delivering babies, and had two daughters of their own. The Bijan Hospital was a four-story building at the end of a nameless dirt road. When the street was finally paved, the city named it after my father. Years later, a Sheraton was built down the street, and slowly this road that butted up against a barren landscape became a coveted address.

It was on the penthouse floor of the Bijan Hospital that my sisters and I grew up. I was born three stories below, in the same operating room where many of my cousins and friends were delivered—a room my father urged us to visit. He had great hopes that we would be inspired to follow his path, but I was terrified by the wailing of women in labor.

In the penthouse, our bedrooms were side by side along a white corridor with bleached terrazzo floors and fluorescent lights. At the far end of the corridor was our living and dining room. We didn't find it odd that muffled moans and the smell of formaldehyde would drift through the vents, but my friends who came to play would gawk at the patients walking the grounds of our *home* in their hospital gowns. At the urging of my mother, the patients even joined us for cake at our birthday parties. One friend was eventually forbidden to come to our house because his mother worried he might catch something.

The nurses doubled as our babysitters. Nurse Aghdas was our favorite, a quasi Mary Poppins with a chipped front tooth. She organized relay races in the corridors, dressed us up as doctors and nurses, taught us first aid, and dispensed bandages and cough lozenges with abandon. And when, at thirteen, I decided to pluck my eyebrows without my mother's consent, she supplied me with the pair of tweezers that I still use today, although she bore my mother's wrath for the gift.

All the bedrooms opened to a long, narrow balcony that faced the hospital gardens. The first day of summer, we moved our beds to the balcony and slept there until the first day of fall. We hauled out the dining room table as well, allowing us to eat summer meals outside. I loved sleeping outdoors, where the sheets on my sunburned shoulders were cool from the night air, where we woke to the sound of Baba the gardener's hacking cough and the spray of his garden hose. I loved the hospital grounds, where I learned to swim in a shallow green pool by tiptoeing farther and farther along its kidney-shaped rim. In the winter when the pool froze, I begged my mother to allow me to go ice-skating, to no avail. Nevertheless, I sat on the edge to let my feet shuffle and glide, gathering the shaved ice with mittened hands for pretend ice cream cones. In spring I scooped up tadpoles in jam jars from its green, murky mush. In early summer, when the pool was drained to be cleaned, Baba hopped in, wearing tall rubber boots. I watched and counted the strokes of his deck brush, listening to the back-and-forth scrape, scrape. It would take him all day to scrub the walls, and by early evening he would climb out, throw a hose over the side, and turn it on full blast. The slow rise and sound of the water continued through my bedtime. I would wake up and lean over the balcony to be the first to see it in the morning light, longing to go for a swim, annoyed by the one or two leaves that already marred its sparkling surface. When my father took the training wheels off my bike, it was around that pool that I rode, with him running alongside.

My father managed to balance his work and family life. The hospital grounds provided us with endless hours of exploration and entertainment. Coming home one day from visiting a patient, he had seen a peddler beating his donkey with a stick. He stopped to reason with the man, but offering to buy the donkey seemed to be the only way to stop the man from abusing it. So he gave him directions to the hospital and drove away, pleased with himself for rescuing the animal *and* providing his children with a pet that they could ride and feed and whose mane they could braid with their mother's knitting yarn. That afternoon, Baba opened the gate to find the peddler and his battered donkey asking for my father. Baba explained that *Doktor* was not a veterinarian, but agreed to call him. By then my father had laid the groundwork for introducing my mother to our new pet: *I couldn't very well stand by and watch an innocent beast beaten, could I?* After paying the peddler, Baba pulled the donkey by the rope around its neck to the garden, where my father lined us up for our surprise. No sooner had Baba shut the gate than the donkey jerked back on the makeshift bridle and snapped at his arm, then turned and bucked, knocking Baba, a lean, six-foot-three man, to the ground. Those two never got along after that. In fact, none of us could go near the ornery animal. My father had rescued him too late. *Can I have a horse instead?* I asked my mother that night. Thus he became my father's pet and was simply named Khar, which means "donkey" in Farsi. For weeks, my father stopped at the greengrocer for wilted heads of lettuce for Khar, prompting satire on social inequality in the local paper by a columnist who had overheard their exchange. The article began, *Ah, to be the pampered ass of Dr. Bijan, with a daily menu of butter lettuce hearts and sugar beet tops, hand-selected by the good doctor himself,* and so on. My mother had had enough. She donated Khar to a park, where the groundskeeper managed to put a saddle on him and offer rides to children for a nickel. A few weeks later, we got a tamer pet: a big black poodle named Sasha. And in winter, my mother knitted him a red turtleneck.

I spent most summer afternoons perched on the branches of the tall sour cherry trees that grew along the garden fence, with my feet dangling, my lips stained red, and a mess of cherry pits below. I hopped down when my mother threatened me with a hospital stay *downstairs*. If I managed to save any cherries for her, she would make sour cherry preserves, syrup to flavor our summer drinks, or, best of all, *albalu polo,* saffron rice with sour cherries, pistachios, and braised game hens. My father kept a vegetable patch tucked in a corner of the garden, where I chased geese and chickens and pulled up turnips and carrots. Under a walnut tree he hung an enormous canopy swing with paisley cushions that had room for all of us. In the summer my mother would serve afternoon tea there with cream puffs or custard-filled doughnuts. She would get up to shake the mulberry tree and we would dance underneath, holding the corners of our skirts, catching the creamy white berries, sweeter than sugar cubes.

My parents threw elaborate parties in the garden, with lambs roasting over fire pits, classical Persian musicians, and tents lined with Persian carpets and lit by lanterns. My mother was famous for her theme parties. For years everyone talked about the fishing party for which she bought live trout and threw them in the pool. Each guest was given a net, and several cleaning and grilling stations were set up. Around the candlelit pool, ladies in evening gowns shimmered like mermaids, all huddled together and giggling over their slippery catch. Their husbands, awkward in rolled-up sleeves, worried about their patent leather shoes and whether they would ever get any dinner. The less lighthearted smoked in the background and nursed their glasses of scotch. I loved these parties. Other than my having to wear a party dress and tame my curls, they were moments of wild independence. I roamed freely among the guests, sampled the éclairs I had longed for all day, eavesdropped, and stole cigarettes from silver trays that accompanied ashtrays like bowls of fancy mixed nuts.

On occasion, my cousin Roya would be at these parties. We were only a year apart, but she was clever and full of ruses, whereas I was far more timid. So she had no choice but to concoct a courage serum for me. She filled my mother's empty bottle of Joy perfume with water and made me take a few swigs before embarking on one of our missions. The serum worked remarkably well. I followed her willingly through cobwebs to the toolshed or the basement in search of clues. We kept our equipment—a compass/nail clipper, a ruler, matches, a notepad and pencil—in a red vinyl drawstring bag. My parents' parties set the perfect stage for our escapades, and with the serum running through my veins, I was a bold inspector and everyone was suspect, including the cook and the gardener.

In the afterglow of these parties—for they really were fairy-tale events—the tents and chairs were folded away, the grounds swept, and the hospital resumed its day-to-day business. The everyday meals at the hospital were prepared by my mother and our cook. The maternity ward was a haven for new mothers, who were encouraged to stay and rest at least a week. My mother coddled them, coaching them through breastfeeding and baby care before sending them home. She would write weekly menus, creating special meals for patients with dietary restrictions, using ingredients that were bought daily at the market or harvested from our garden. The same dishes served to the patients on trays lined with starched white linen and garden roses, we ate upstairs on our dining room table, family-style.

My mother also brought her stringent medical training to the kitchen, dismissing cooks who lacked organizational skills, were messy, or simply weren't liked by her children. One ill-fated cook, Ahmed Agha, came from the Hilton Hotel with excellent references. He prepared a trial meal for my parents that ended with a pomegranate sorbet, which sent my mother into raptures. She hired him on the spot. In the weeks that followed, my sisters launched a campaign to bring poor Ahmed Agha down simply because he forbade us access to the kitchen. Even my mother prefaced her forays into the kitchen with apologies and compliments. Days after his arrival, pebbles appeared in my sisters' meals. At first my parents hesitated to mention anything to their new chef, but by the third night, when my sisters were lining up rocks on the edge of their plates, my father called him upstairs to explain his oversight. Ahmed turned purple and apologized, promising to be more careful when washing and sorting the vegetables and legumes. My sisters claimed round one. By the next evening, two screaming girls were dragged upstairs to the dining room. Ahmed Agha held my sisters by the back of their frocks and roared, *Madam, I have caught the saboteurs!* He had suspected mischief and followed them to the garden before dinner, where he watched them load their pockets with pebbles en route to the table. My parents stared in disbelief as he ordered their daughters to empty their pockets. Once the pebbles started hitting the ground, he untied his apron and draped it over the back of a chair with great flourish. He announced his resignation, though he alerted my mother to a cauliflower soufflé in the oven. My sisters hung their heads and stared at their shoes. They had still won.

Until a new cook was found, my mother did double duty, and once again the kitchen door remained open. One minute she would be stirring a pot of stew, and the next she was being called to the ER. She made this transition smoothly, turning the stove off, securing her nursing cap with hairpins, and washing up before jogging down the corridors to join my father.

When I wandered into the kitchen, I would hover around my mother until she gave me a task, washing the fruit she had bought at the market, arranging the patient trays, peeling, chopping. My mother never waved me away to go play outside, but rather expected me to keep in step, giving me patient instructions with the confidence that I would carry them through. We enjoyed each other's company while we sorted through a sack of lentils or shucked beans. When I did my homework, I liked nothing better than to work quietly at the kitchen table as she moved from pantry to sink to stove, breaking the silence only to ask her a question I already knew

the answer to, just to hear her voice and feel connected to
her task.

When it was time to set the table, my mother would remind us about the particularities of my father's place setting.
He required his own *mise en place*—a tomato, a cucumber,
a tender lettuce heart, a lemon, salt, a pepper mill, and olive
oil. He preferred to make a salad for one at the table, where
he could slice and season *à la minute*. We watched him every
night peeling his cucumber, dicing his tomato, dressing his
salad, and puckering with the first taste, which convinced us
that what he had was better than the salad my mother had
made. We gladly accepted his offer of lemony bites. My parents nourished us with lavash bread from the oven wrapped
around sheep's-milk cheese with fresh walnuts and just-picked
tarragon, figs in season, buttery lamb shanks with fava beans
and saffron-scented rice, cantaloupes spooned into chilled
bowls and drizzled with rose water. They brought these to
us as if for the first time. At times quarrelsome or tired, they
were all enthusiasm when we were hungry.

Our routine would change with the seasons. In the summer we began our meals with a chilled, minty cucumber and
yogurt soup. To my delight, my mother left me in charge of
this soup the summer I turned eight. I loved the little varia-
tions I could make, substituting torn rose petals for mint,
adding raisins and crushed walnuts, or ice cubes with mint
leaves frozen inside on particularly hot, dusty Tehran days.

But regardless of the time of year, we always ended a meal

with a bowl of seasonal fruits, chosen carefully by my parents on their daily market run. Few Iranians can walk past a fruit stall without lingering a moment to fondle a melon or sample a grape. One of my beloved chores was to wash the fruit they brought home in a shallow tub of cold, soapy water with a soft sponge, then rinse and pat it dry before placing it tenderly in a bowl—a still life I painstakingly arranged. The fruit was served whole, and one had to know how to properly eat a persimmon, peel an orange, section an apple and offer some around the table. Ceremony was a big part of our meals. We may not have prayed every day, but gratitude was an essential component of every gathering at the table.

Pomegranate Granita

. . . .

My mother never forgot the taste of that pomegranate sorbet that got Ahmed Agha the job at the hospital. As the years went by, she mused about the texture and balance of that sorbet. I was inspired by her longing to experiment with pomegranate desserts, and this "shaved ice" was my answer to her bygone chef's masterpiece.

Serves 4

2 cups pomegranate juice, fresh squeezed or bottled, unsweetened
1½ cups simple syrup (see following recipe)

1. In a large bowl, whisk together the pomegranate juice and the simple syrup. Pour the pomegranate mixture into a 9-inch shallow pan and put it in the freezer.

2. Every ½ hour or so, stir the mixture up delicately with the tines of a fork to break up the ice crystals that form around the edge of the pan, giving the granita a light texture and preventing it from freezing into a solid block.

3. Freeze the granita 6 to 8 hours. It is best served the day it is made. To serve, shave the frozen mixture with a spoon into chilled parfait glasses. Garnish with mint and pomegranate seeds.

Simple Syrup

Yields 2 cups

2 cups sugar
¾ cup water
Zest of 1 lemon
2 to 3 sprigs fresh mint

In a small pot, mix the sugar and water together with the lemon
zest and mint. Bring to a boil. Simmer 2 minutes. Discard the
mint sprigs. Remove the pot from heat and cool. Simple syrup
will keep for weeks in the refrigerator and is handy for sweeten-
ing iced tea or lemonade.

Sour Cherry Upside-Down Cake

Cakes and cookies were a rare treat when I was little. On special occasions, when I was allowed to choose a pastry, I never fancied rich, creamy confections, preferring the simple, unadorned cakes. Even today I'll take a piece of pound cake over a frosted layer cake. One of my favorites, which my mother would buy for me with great ceremony, was a cardamom cupcake that could be found in any ordinary bakery.

My attempts to re-create this childhood treat resulted in an upside-down cake with caramelized sour cherries. As a child, I spent hours dangling from the branches of the sour cherry trees that lined the hospital grounds, but I ate most of what I picked. These days, I wait for the two weeks in July when a few markets have fresh sour cherries, and I buy as many as I can to make preserves or freeze. However, this cake works beautifully with Bing cherries, red or yellow plums, or apricots when they are plentiful and in season. The tart fruit juices seep into the cardamom cake, and it's difficult not to steal bites every time you walk by.

Serves 8 to 10

Sour Cherry Compote

5 tablespoons unsalted butter

1 cup firmly packed brown sugar

2 cups pitted sour cherries, fresh if available, otherwise substitute
   with Bing cherries, ripe plums, or apricots

Cardamom Cake

4 tablespoons unsalted butter

1 cup brown sugar

1½ cups flour

2 teaspoons baking powder

½ teaspoon ground cardamom

½ teaspoon salt

½ cup half-and-half

1 teaspoon vanilla extract

2 large eggs

1. Butter and flour a 9-inch round cake pan.

2. To make the sour cherry compote, melt the butter in a small saucepan and stir in the brown sugar. With a rubber spatula, gently fold in the sour cherries and pour into the bottom of your cake pan. Set aside.

3. Preheat the oven to 350°F.

4. To make the cardamom cake, cream together the butter and the sugar in the bowl of an electric mixer until fluffy.

5. Sift together the flour, baking powder, cardamom, and salt. Add to the creamed butter alternately with the half-and-half and mix until smooth.

6. Add the vanilla extract and the eggs one by one. Continue mixing just until the batter is combined.

7. Pour the batter on top of the cherries. Place the cake in the center of the oven and bake for 45 minutes, until a toothpick inserted in the middle comes out clean.

8. Remove the cake from the oven. Allow to cool for 5 minutes. Run a knife along the edge of the cake pan before inverting the cake onto a platter. Don't worry if the fruit doesn't fall over the cake; it's happened to me a million times. Simply scoop the cherries and spread evenly over the cake. Serve warm with pistachio ice cream.

Chapter 2

IN THE SUMMER of 1978, I was fifteen years old and I had left Iran with my parents for a vacation in Spain and a reunion with my two sisters, who were attending college in the United States. We had arrived on the island of Majorca with little more than beachwear, paperback books, and a backgammon set, with the intention of staying for a month in a studio apartment.

My father often woke up early to buy our morning bread. He was friendly with the merchants on the busy street lined with bakeries, cafés, money-exchange booths, and souvenir shops that catered to summer tourists. The buxom lady at the butcher's beamed whenever he strolled in, anticipating their animated exchange without words, for my father didn't speak Spanish. Relying on farm-animal pantomime, they managed to fill his shopping bag with the day's meal:

Buenos días, Doktor!
Buenos días, señora!
Baa-baa bien? (Hand on his shoulder.)
Sí, sí, Doktor, baa-baa muy bien!

Once she had selected and weighed a lamb shoulder roast for him, she would wipe her broad hands excitedly on her apron before handing him his parcel. They would wave good-bye and my father would present the roast with great pride to my mother. Expecting his return, she would be in the kitchen frying up the onions for our lunch, humming along with the radio.

My father took great pleasure in his shopping expeditions, and my mother was happy to indulge him, sending him out even for a single tomato. He would return weighed down with shopping bags. The kitchen in our tiny apartment was already stocked with jars of Hero jam, cans of Spanish olives, braids of pimientos and garlic to last many seasons. Unpacking the bags, she shook her head from side to side and muttered to herself, adding another can of sardines to the row below and rinsing the purple figs he handed to her almost apologetically.

Unlike most families, who look forward to vacations as an opportunity to eat out, our family enjoyed finding good markets and making our meals with the local ingredients while on holiday. My father did not trust restaurants, imagining them as petri dishes where bacteria flourished. When we traveled, he brought along the equivalent of a well-stocked first aid kit—albeit gourmand—with an assortment of knives, corkscrews, can openers, salt and pepper mills, minibottles of mustard, olive oil, scotch, and vodka, and occasionally caviar. Beluga caviar traveled with us packed in oily blue tins (the cans were so chock-full that fish oil inevitably seeped out) wrapped in ice packs, two or three for gifts, and one for us, which we ceremoniously opened upon on our arrival. If we were hungry, my father simply gave us a spoon and we ate it like jam, but he preferred to wait until he was set up, easily transforming the desk in any hotel room into a kitchenette. No sooner had we checked in than he would pop open his suitcase, set up the "bar," and call room service for ice and lemon. Soon after, he would scour the neighborhood for delis, charcuteries, bakeries, stocking up on local groceries. This foraging was as essential as sightseeing. The cathedrals and museums were impressive, but he was curious about what the locals ate, their markets, their shopping carts. Eating out was an ice cream cone, or a cold Coke at a sidewalk café, and you could always count on my parents to have mints, chocolates, or lemon drops in their coat pockets when your feet hurt and you couldn't bear to see another ruin. I remember what a big deal it was when in Rome my mother took us out for a pizza while my father made an excuse to go to a travel agency to check on our tickets. Refusing tourist meals, he would reason with us that having followed the locals, he had found the best mortadella studded with pistachios, crusty bread, mountain cheese, and exquisite plums. *Let's go back to our room, where*

I will serve you first zakuski. He favored this Russian term for appetizers. *I have green olives stuffed with peppers, white asparagus with aioli, and of course caviar on toast with a squeeze of lemon. And is not that far better than a bowl of cold spaghetti the man boiled in his shoe?* My father referred to all restaurateurs, as *the man.* Back in our hotel room, perched on the edge of our beds, he sliced ripe tomatoes, sprinkled them with salt, and fed us like baby birds.

Our apartment in Majorca had a balcony wide enough for three narrow cots, where my sisters and I slept. In the next room, my parents made their bed on a pullout couch. My father's thunderous snoring kept us up late into the night, but it was my opportunity to plead with my sisters for stories about college life and boyfriends. I imagined them living inside an *Archie* comic book, where girls plotted, boys were clueless, and they gathered at the soda fountain to eat cheeseburgers and work it out. When my sisters tired of my queries—*Yes, you can order a hamburger and eat it in your car. No, I don't have a date every Saturday night. Now, GO TO SLEEP!*—I pulled the sheet over my head and read Agatha Christie and Georges Simenon mysteries that my mother had finished and passed along, still uncertain what exactly went on in college.

In the morning I heard my father latch the door on his way out to the bakery. My mother stirred, then woke up swiftly. I rolled over and watched her plump their pillows and fold the light summer blankets, storing them neatly in the drawer

under the couch. I'd tap on the sliding glass door that separated us and she would push her morning hair away from her
face and look up with a smile, then gesture to me that she was
going to the kitchen to put the kettle on. We rose one by one,
put away our bedding, set the breakfast table, then took turns
brushing our teeth and slipping on bathing suits, moving to
the quiet rhythm of another lazy day, unaware that these few
weeks would be the last time the five of us would be together
in this unfettered way.

My father returned with a large *ensaimada,* still warm and
dusted with powdered sugar. It's a Majorcan specialty, and I
had seen travelers at the airport carrying stacks of them tied
with string to folks back home. For some, Majorca may evoke
a longing for pearls, but for me, it was that light, braided loaf
that left a trace of sugar on my lips, and the slow sweeping
of the sweet flakes with my fingertips from the greasy box it
came in.

My mother carried the breakfast tray with jars of jam and
slices of melon. I followed her with the percolator and a pitcher
of steamed milk. Perched around a table on the balcony, with
glasses of *café con leche,* we ate our breakfast in our bathing
suits and planned another slow day on the rocky beach. In the
evenings you would find us there again, the Mediterranean a
thin blue band in the far distance, and a row of bright swim-
suits drying on the railing. Music from nearby discotheques
would fill the air, and my sisters would sway or sing along with

the Bee Gees' "Stayin' Alive" and ABBA's "Take a Chance on Me." They were so cool that I felt my own status elevated just being in their shadow, watching them to learn their moves, mouthing the lyrics or at least the words I could grasp. Showered and darker than yesterday, we played backgammon and nibbled on olives and pistachios while my father nursed a whiskey soda and my mother fiddled with the radio.

Surrounded by tourists, mostly Brits with sunburns, we kept to ourselves, preferring the slow pace of our meals, our strolls into town, window shopping for shoes, and the occasional ice cream at a sidewalk café. I was never a zealous shopper—unless it was for food. I preferred to linger over a dish of coffee ice cream rather than slip on an endless array of leather jackets and bikinis, but my adolescent awe for my sisters was a powerful draw. If they asked for my opinion on a color or style, my chest would swell like a pigeon's, urging them to hold it up one more time while my mind hastened to call a verdict: *Go with the blue. It matches your eyes.* But what did I know? I felt compelled to accompany them on their excursions, admiring their poise and mimicking their taste for clothes and makeup—seduced, really, by the scent of the lotions and lip gloss they carried from America. My teenage angst made me awkward and self-aware, so I looked to them for reassurance:

This suit makes me look fat.
No, it's pretty.

I think I should get one with vertical lines.

No, I like the polka dots.

Polka dots are for babies! I'm almost sixteen, you know!

Despite the assurances from my mother and sisters that my hair was curly, not *frizzy*, that my nose had character and was not *like a coat hook*, that my glasses made me look smart, not *nerdy*, I wasn't convinced. I rounded my shoulders and observed boys from inside my shell. We were hardly mischievous. A threatening frown from my mother was usually enough warning. I once joined some kids who were going to a club. I drank vodka and orange juice, then slow-danced to Julio Iglesias with a Spanish boy who smelled of Chaps and cigarettes and came up to my shoulders. When a taxi dropped me off that evening, my father was waiting for me in the hallway with clenched fists. My sisters found it unfair that I was given liberties denied to them at fifteen. I wanted to shout and tell them where I had been, that vodka made my skin tingle, that a Spanish boy had held me, that he had chosen *me—me*, with the frizzy hair and the square windowpane glasses on a hooked nose. But instead I shrugged it off and took my place around the table to pick up the hand that was dealt for me, joining the late-night gin rummy game.

Day after day seemed the same, yet things were shifting. Through the whistle and static on BBC Radio, we heard news of scattered protests on the streets of Tehran against the monarchy. Although we were aware of these skirmishes, the newscasts were increasingly alarming as riots gained momentum and spread to major cities. Demonstrators were on a rampage, bombing establishments that symbolized Western decadence: liquor stores, nightclubs, cinemas, even schools attended by foreign students. It seemed our country was unraveling at terrific speed as we listened to reports of widespread bloodshed and violence. There, perched on a Spanish island, in relative calm, I couldn't grasp the chaos that spilled from the radio. It seemed far away, and I think even my parents, despite mounting evidence, thought, *Surely, this can't last.*

The tone of our evenings became somber, a dark mood overtaking our carefree days like an uninvited guest, without apology or departure date, hovering over our backgammon games, more tedious now than playful. The grooves on my father's forehead ran deep, and an unlit cigarette often twitched at the corner of his mouth. He didn't even smoke. If my mother wasn't adjusting the antenna on the radio, my father held it on his lap, coaxing better reception. They'd continue to follow the news long after we had gone to bed. Their vigilance cast a shadow on our bright mornings, they only half listened to my teenage gripes and didn't bother correcting my posture or rubbing suntan lotion on my back.

The urgent call we received from my uncle was unexpected. His news was of an upheaval on a much larger scale, with the imminent fall of the Shah. Across the rattle of telephone lines, he warned us not to return to Iran. We listened to his news with numb disbelief as riots exploded in our country, and every day brought reports of another friend captured as crowds marched with a boldness never before seen under the rule of the Shah.

Having held public office and championed women's rights, my mother was an obvious target of the Islamic revolutionaries sweeping the country. If she were to return, her fate in the hands of Khomeini's followers would be to stand before his Revolutionary Guards and be showered with bullets—the picture of her slain body posted next to all the other "enemies of the revolution" on the pages of their newspapers.

Subsequent phone calls revealed that our home had been seized, our assets frozen, and our relatives interrogated. With this news came the recognition that we might be exiled indefinitely. Having already harbored some resentment toward his wife for her political aspirations, my father, seeking someone to blame for our loss, turned his anger toward my mother. He mocked her efforts on behalf of the Iranian women now marching shoulder to shoulder with their Muslim brothers. The injustices she had fought, and a lifetime of hard-won legislation, were erased with the swift swipe of a cleric's cape.

With the school year about to begin, my sisters returned to America to resume their studies. My mother took a tour of the local high school in Palma and made arrangements with the principal for my registration. I resisted her plans and persuaded her to let me join my best friend, Neda, who was already attending a boarding school in Michigan. Amid the turmoil in my family, I heard America's call clearly. Within weeks, we took the ferry to Barcelona to apply for my student visa at the U.S. Consulate, and I made the decision to leave my parents behind. At the time it seemed obvious to me that sooner or later I would be sent to college abroad, so going a few years earlier than planned wouldn't make a difference. I was restless with anticipation of a life in the United States, regarding it like spending the summer with a glamorous cousin. Ironic, really, a teenager assuming control over her future when all other assumptions are dispelled. In hindsight, I am astonished at my shallow take on the massive upheaval that overturned my country and the lives of its people—as if I weren't a part of it—and incredulous that my parents felt utterly powerless, even to curb their daughter's foolhardy yearning for America.

We celebrated my sixteenth birthday on the balcony, now our place of refuge. My father let me win several rounds of backgammon. The butcher had selected a nice, plump chicken for my mother to make one of my favorite dishes with saffron yogurt rice. During my last week she had made all my preferred meals, in a prescient and feverish preparation for a premature good-bye to her youngest daughter. The mood had shifted from somber to resigned. I know my mother's heart was breaking, but she wouldn't let me see her cry. Maybe my parents had convinced themselves that allowing me to leave was proof of their confidence in me, the only sure thing in the face of uncertainty, but most likely they were simply stunned. I don't know because I never asked, ashamed to this day of my selfish pursuit. The morning of my departure, we shared our last *ensaimada* with dollops of my mother's homemade quince and carrot marmalade. My parents would spend the next year as refugees, biding their time, waiting for the dust of the revolution to settle. But the dust became a storm that left their lives in ruins.

Saffron Yogurt Rice with Chicken and Eggplant

* *

Equally delicious with braised lamb shanks, the saffron and yogurt marinade is essential to the subtle tartness of this dish, with egg yolks used as a binding for the rice. For serving, the ta-chin is turned out onto a serving dish and cut into square pieces, as one would cut a cake. As a child, I found this resemblance to yellow cake very appealing.

Serves 6

4 free-range chicken breasts and 4 thighs, boneless, skin on

3 cups Greek yogurt

Zest and juice of 2 lemons and 1 orange

1 teaspoon ground saffron dissolved in ⅓ cup hot water

3 cups basmati rice

2 globe eggplants or 5 Japanese eggplants

5 tablespoons olive oil

4 egg yolks

6 ounces (1½ sticks) butter, melted

1 teaspoon cinnamon

Kosher salt and fresh-ground pepper

1. Marinate the chicken overnight in a mixture of the yogurt, lemon and orange juice and peel, dissolved saffron, kosher salt, and fresh-ground pepper.

2. Soak the rice in water (enough to cover by 1 inch) and 1 table-spoon of salt for 2 to 3 hours.

3. Preheat the oven to 350°F.

4. Wash and peel the eggplants and slice them lengthwise ¼ inch thick. Line a baking sheet with parchment paper brushed with olive oil and overlap the slices of eggplant in a single layer. Brush the eggplant with olive oil, season with salt and pepper, and bake for 20 to 25 minutes, until tender. Remove from the oven and cool.

5. Remove the chicken from the marinade and save the yogurt mixture in the refrigerator. Heat 2 tablespoons of olive oil and brown the chicken pieces on both sides in an oven-proof skillet over medium-high heat. Place the skillet in the oven and bake the chicken for 20 minutes. Remove from the oven and set aside, reserving any juices from the pan.

6. Boil 2 quarts of water with 1 tablespoon of salt in a large non-stick pot. Wash and drain the rice, then pour into the boiling water. Boil for 8 minutes, stirring once or twice, then strain.

7. Whisk together the yogurt marinade with the egg yolks. In a large bowl, gently combine the rice with the yogurt mixture to coat the rice but not break the grains.

8. Pour half the melted butter into a 14-inch ovenproof dish. Place a layer of yogurt rice on the bottom, then a layer of egg-plant, cover the eggplant with another layer of rice, and place

the chicken pieces on top. Continue with a layer each of rice, eggplant, and chicken, finishing with a layer of rice. Sprinkle with the remaining butter, cinnamon, and chicken juices. Pat gently with a spatula and cover with foil.

9. Place on the middle rack of the preheated oven and bake 2 hours. If using a glass dish, you will be able to see when the bottom turns golden.

10. Remove from the oven and keep covered until ready to serve. Using the edge of a metal spatula, loosen the baked edges. Hold a serving dish over the baking dish and turn over to unmold the rice.

My Mother's Quince Marmalade
. . . .

*It is inevitable that when I'm selecting quinces at the market, people
will ask me,* What are these, apples? *or* What do you mean you
have to cook them to eat them? *Their lumpy, pale yellow skin will
often prompt,* Are you sure they're not pears? *I'll hold one up to
their nose and watch their eyes open wide with wonder. So fragrant
are these ancient fruit of the Middle East that at room temperature,
they perfume your entire house. Far too sour to be eaten raw, when
they are cooked slowly with sugar, their natural pectin transforms
them into beautiful preserves with a rosy hue. In Iran they are
combined with fatty meat dishes like lamb stew to counteract the
richness, adding a sweet-tart complexity. In Moroccan cuisine
they are incorporated into tagines laced with clove and cinnamon.
Quince paste is made widely in Europe and has become a frequent
accompaniment to cheese in America. I'm on the lookout for quinces
in our local markets from October to January.*

*This marmalade is delightful spread on scones or whole wheat
toast, tucked into a crepe, or served as an accompaniment to goat
cheese or Spanish Manchego.*

2 pounds quinces
1 pound carrots
4 crushed cardamom pods
5 cups sugar
1 cup water
2 lemons, zest and juice
1 orange, zest and juice

1. Peel and shred the quince and carrots using a grater or a food processor. Combine well. Save ½ tablespoon of quince seeds and wrap them in a piece of cheesecloth with the crushed cardamom pods.

2. Place the carrots and quince in a large, heavy-bottomed saucepan, then add the sugar, water, lemon and orange juice and zest, and the quince seed and cardamom pouch. Stir to coat the shredded carrots and quince.

3. Bring to a boil, skimming any foam off the surface. Reduce the heat to low and simmer, stirring gently every once in a while for 2 hours, or until the marmalade is glossy and syrupy thick. Remove the seed pouch.

4. Fill jelly jars with the hot marmalade and seal them. Keep in the refrigerator or in a cool, dark pantry.

Chapter 3

I COULD ARGUE that I had been preparing to leave long before the cries of revolution. When I was seven, my father had given me a white vinyl Pan Am bag, a souvenir from a trip abroad. I packed this bag with essentials that I thought I would need in case I was ever kidnapped. Odd as this may seem, it was my "disaster kit," complete with a pair of clean white socks, underwear, a stuffed rabbit, a tin of cookies, color pencils, and a notebook. From time to time and over the years, I refreshed the contents, exchanging the rabbit for a Barbie, or underwear for the next size. I believed that if I ever needed to leave in a hurry, I would politely ask my captors permission to grab my bag. My parents never knew I had it, but I always thought they would have been proud of me for being prepared.

Thinking back to my departure from Spain, I have often tried to put myself in my mother's shoes the day she put me on that plane to New York. How did she go back to that apartment where my bathing suit still hung to dry on the balcony railing? With so little regard for the gravity of their situation, how could I have left her alone with that emptiness and uncertainty, and with an angry, bitter husband to contend with? My country was exploding and I was preoccupied with blue jean styles.

As I began my junior year at an American high school, it was fortunate that I spoke English and was easily able to follow the curriculum. Neda's family invited me to stay with them, an extraordinarily generous offer, thus saving my parents an outstanding expense and rescuing me from becoming a boarder. Neda's mother brought me under her wing and looked after me like her own child for two years. I was introduced to Christmas, Halloween, and Easter, marveling at the elaborate products that accompanied each holiday. Intimidated by the scale of preparations, I worried whether I would ever observe them without being so obviously clueless, but my friend and her family taught me the rituals and included me in all their festivities. I learned to paint my face and walk around the neighborhood in the dark with a pillowcase in hand and ask for candy. I learned to wrap gifts and make bows, to stay in my pajamas on Christmas morning, to eat my turkey with cranberry jelly, and to look for painted eggs in bushes. On Thanksgiving, I discovered pie. Until then, I had only known apple pie, but Neda's grandmother baked rhubarb, sour cherry, pumpkin, and peach, taking each out of the oven just when the fruit was bubbling around the edges. Not surprisingly, it became my favorite holiday and the beginning of a lifelong passion for pie.

The social arena was a different matter. Having carefully studied old issues of *Seventeen* magazine, courtesy of my sisters studying abroad, I thought I had a fairly good handle on the American high school culture. But nowhere in any of those advice columns were the issues of a foreign student from a hostile country addressed. The tips regarding how to be popular, or how to make the boys notice you, were useless when all I wanted was to be *unnoticed* and to blend in. I didn't understand yet the correlation between belonging and blending in. My true sense of belonging was lost forever, along with my dog, my stamp collection, my charm bracelet, my house, my street, my school, my country.

In Iran, I had attended an international school with a bilingual curriculum and a student body resembling the UN. Our science, math, and social studies were taught in English, and humanities, poetry, and literature, in Farsi. On the playground we came together from every corner of the globe, and we thought it was so everywhere. It was a remarkable introduction to history and geography. Friendships were based on curiosity—we were all foreigners to one another, our cultural diversities a kind of splendor. But if you were a foreign student in a relatively homogeneous private school in the Midwest, especially one from a country that was covered in the nightly news as a *former* ally of the United States, where its citizens were shown marching to the tune of *America, the Great Satan,* blindfolding and taking hostage U.S. Embassy employees, well, then, you weren't going to blend into a coterie of jocks, punks, or preps. You didn't even understand exactly what separated them, except for their clothes, because after all, they all came from the same place.

Nevertheless, just a few miles away from the multinational amity of my school, in the south of Tehran, a neighborhood I had only glimpsed through a car window on our way to weekly lunches at my grandfather's house, children who did not benefit from these opportunities stewed in a pressure cooker stirred by clerics shunned by the Shah. These children accompanied their parents to Friday prayers while I took ski lessons in the Alborz Mountains. I sung the words to "This Land Is Your Land" and "La Marseillaise"; they memorized verses from the Koran. While we begged our parents for mini-skirts, they tightened the knots on their headscarves. And while these families observed the Islamic holidays, I wanted to know all about Santa Claus. We were just a few miles away, yet we might as well have been on the moon.

What I knew of America, I had learned from the American students and teachers at my old school. I had observed their confidence—their slouch as they sat at their desks with their long legs stretched out defiantly. An Iranian student would simply not sit this way unless he was mimicking a gesture he wished to own. I envied their athleticism, in awe of the grace-ful ease with which they pitched a ball, dove into a pool, or tossed a basketball. I admired how naturally they stored and cataloged sports trivia without engaging in the rote memorization we were accustomed to. They could not recite Hafez by heart, but they knew multiple baseball scores from games lost or won years ago. Most of all, from their bold and candid inquiries, I learned how to construct and voice a question, and how to distinguish a real answer from oratory, which my Iranian teachers had mastered. And I marveled at the frank and open-ended discussions in the classroom with my American teachers, who challenged knowledge I had thought absolute.

In Tehran, when I was invited to play in the homes of my American classmates, I took inventory of their cereals, maple syrup, and cake mixes, their glossy hair products and magnificent lip gloss collections, their denim, and the smell of their laundry soap, all stocked from the commissary—an elusive store we had no access to. What struck me was how long you could be in someone's home before anyone offered you a glass of water (we were taught never to ask for anything). In an Iranian home, you are fed fifteen times before the mud on your shoes dries. My friend Sally would burst through the front door of her house yelling, *Mom! What's there to eat?* No tray with the afternoon snack was set on the table. I stared bewildered as she grazed standing up, the milk bottle to her mouth. She tried to teach me a lesson in survival: *If you want something, you go into the kitchen, open the refrigerator door, and get it yourself.* This idea was so preposterous, I thought she was trying to get me in trouble with her mother. If someone had walked into our house and helped himself, my mother would have been outraged that we had not prepared the tea tray. Food and drink were to be offered preemptively to any man, woman, or child who rang the doorbell, and accepted graciously after a long, convoluted exchange:

> Really, I've just had lunch.
> Just a taste. It's my special rhubarb compote.
> No, thank you. I'm running late.
> Late for what? Come in, come in. I've just made some tea.

And so on, until the guest relented and they might, at last, have a real conversation.

Playing Barbie with my cousins who had moved to Iran from California with a trunkful of flashy accessories, plus a Ken, I had learned about the rituals of courting American-style: dating, movies, popcorn, soda fountains, jukeboxes, convertibles, and the necessary wardrobe for a girl on the go. When they had had enough and begged me to play a different game, I staged a vote and enforced my will upon my younger cousins—writing "Barbie" on all the ballots before folding them and asking them to pick from a hat. I thought I was so clever. Of course they knew I was strong-arming them, but they sweetly consented and we staged another rendezvous with Ken. I never tired of Barbie's freedom to turn down invitations, to help herself to popcorn and soda, and to accept gifts and compliments without indebtedness.

I was in love with an America that I believed was not weighed down with the anchors of custom. I envied the absence of formality and rigid cultural codes of behavior. Their nihilism was a vast, open plain to the complexities of my Persian landscape.

Yet here I was, and after all that longing for America, I was surprised by how much I missed home. I had dreamt of America for so long, but when I finally arrived, I found it was just a place where people lived, worked, took their children to school. Initially, what seemed exotic were the sloping, manicured green lawns, the quaint mailboxes with their red flags, and the chipmunks—in Tehran you never saw wild animals scurrying about your yard. And it wasn't long before I was seduced by the dizzying array of food: Thirty-six flavors of ice cream, thirty-six! Sundaes and milk shakes: small, medium, large? Large, of course! With or without whipped cream? With, with! Cereals, candy bars, treats made out of cereal and marshmallows, McDonald's hot apple pies! I was ravenous for the food that came out of drive-through windows, the stacks of pancakes and the caddy of syrups, the tubs of popcorn, cheese that squirted out of tubes and melted on salty chips. I could never get enough. Even the mashed potatoes that the homely school cafeteria ladies dished out using ice cream scoops and plopped next to the meat and gravy they called stroganoff intrigued me. I had to taste it all, and eventually I couldn't button my prize jeans. Food offered enormous consolation for homesickness, as well as a chance to make friends, joining amiable classmates at the diner for coffee and cigarettes with buttered raisin toast and jam in foil packages.

I kept my homesickness coiled inside me and concentrated on behaving like my peers, smoking cigarettes to show I wasn't such a dork, listening to learn what they found funny or gross. I wrote long, brave letters to my parents filled with false anecdotes about my triumphs at school and ease with my new classmates, sometimes elaborating on the snacks or a movie Neda's mom had taken us to see. *Grease* had left such an impression on me that for weeks I couldn't get the songs and mannerisms out of my head. At the time, I knew nothing about the relevance of the era when the story took place. I thought this glimpse into high school culture taught me everything I needed to know about jocks, preps, class rings, and cheerleaders, and I expressed as much in my letters.

My parents wrote back equally long and encouraging letters, never once revealing their despair. What good was it to write of my yearning or my awkward status as the foreign student from the dark country of flag-burning hostage takers? Our infrequent telephone conversations were brief, and we stifled our grief even when my mother called with news of my grandfather's death. I pressed the phone to my ear: *Your grandpa died, honey. Baba bozorg is gone.* It seemed impossible that a man who had been surrounded by family and friends all his life had died alone in Iran. Heartsick following my grandmother's death when I was just six, he had learned to live alone, but not a day had gone by without a call or a visit from his daughter, until her exile. And now she could not go back to bury him. His housekeeper of forty years had embraced the revolution that had given her family free *ash,* a hearty noodle soup, to yell *Death to America!* in the streets (rumor was that the regime offered soup to busloads of people if they would join the demonstrations in support of Khomeini). In a zealous reversal of roles, she moved her family into my grandfather's house.

My grandfather had written me a letter that had taken weeks to arrive. It had been opened and read, then carelessly taped and sent once the "sons of the revolution" had established that he was not conspiring to overthrow the republic. I kept it in a shoe box with my parents' letters. I read it again because it was the only tangible object that remained of him, tracing his elegant handwriting. What was missing was his humor, for the content was stoic, encouraging me to focus on my studies and get good marks, to practice my French verbs, and to write letters in Farsi. I imagine he'd written similarly restrained letters to my mother when she was a student far from home, navigating her life in a new country: *Listen to Matron. Save your money. Don't ride your bicycle at night.*

Iran was slipping away from me too fast, taking the shape of a film rather than a real place where I had once dug holes on its sandy beaches and chased pigeons in my grandfather's courtyard. When I'd eaten ice cream under the cool shade of his pergola, where sweetbriar and jasmine tangled in a rivalry of scent, when I'd splashed my cousins from his fountain with the turquoise tiles that held a hand's depth of water, when we'd put on a play of "Rumpelstiltskin" on the stage he had had built for us in his living room, with red velvet curtains and gold tassels, I hadn't known I wouldn't be back.

NEAR THE END of my senior year I had figured out how to maintain an interior and an exterior life. I mimicked my peers by day and by night. I took refuge in the room I shared with Neda, keeping it tidy, ironing my jeans, and doing homework. I pushed away thoughts of home, but they raced to catch me. Sometimes in my dreams I'd be on my bed in my old room, or in the hallways of my school, looking for my locker. I would wake up almost happy to have visited these places in my sleep. I discovered Roth, Bellow, and Malamud in a Jewish American literature class taught by a teacher who went by his first name and brought his dog, an aloof Afghan, to our classroom. We sat on sofas and discussed alienation— a topic I could certainly grasp but failed to find the words for until I went to bed and lay awake with furious debates raging in my head, desperate to bring forth ideas with such command as the authors I was reading. My fury found voice in the stories I wrote for my creative writing class, taught by a beloved teacher who pedaled languidly to school with his trouser cuffs pinned up, his right arm weighed down with a bulging leather briefcase that held our handwritten narratives. His warm voice mediated our alternating admiration and criticism of one another's work. Being susceptible to flattery, I hung on to his praise and his suggestion to submit my work to the student literary magazine. When it came time to fill out college applications, I was suddenly aware that, other than those few entries, my credentials lagged in comparison to those of my classmates. My application lacked tales of debate clubs, yearbook staff, lacrosse teams, chess, choir, track and field.

My parents were filling out applications, too. After a year of living like nomads, waiting to go home, they realized they were never going back to Iran and began applying for visas to America to be near their children. The fact that my mother had relatives in California, and that her brother had earlier married my lovely American aunt, facilitated their decision where to go and also eased the process of acquiring visas. The uncertainty had broken them down, causing them to reel between hope and despair. The only certainty lay in their fate if they returned home: death before a firing squad and three orphaned daughters. The revolution had overturned the very soil where they had laid deep roots, built a life, done good work. They learned that an accomplished past meant nothing to the gentleman behind the desk at the embassy. Their past was no longer relevant, and the winds of change swept them up like the last fall leaves clinging to a branch that has no use for them. They continued to follow the news that drew a grim picture of what had become of their country. The monarchy had collapsed; Khomeini had returned to Iran to become the

Supreme Leader of the Islamic Republic. Armed Revolutionary Guards combed the streets, making random arrests and
executing anyone with a prior connection to the regime. The
news was their only link to a revolution that was not theirs.

In June 1980, with an acceptance to the University of California at Santa Cruz, I reunited with my parents in Fresno,
where my mother had extended family. My parents furnished
their little apartment with lamps, tables, pots, and pans from
yard sales, gradually collecting things to call their own. While
my mother sewed curtains, my father rewired lamps and up-
holstered chairs. They were nesting all over again. Only this
time, there was no heirloom silver, crystal, or carpets. There
were mugs with the logo of the local bank where they had
deposited the meager sum my uncle in Iran had managed to
wire them. But we were safe and we were together.

Once the drapes were hung, my parents quickly set about
acquiring driver's licenses and social security cards and studying for the state medical board exams. They spent numerous
hours poring over DMV manuals and quizzing each other on
road rules. My father was sixty-one. He had been a successful
surgeon and obstetrician in Iran, but as hard as he studied
the medical textbooks, the nuances of the English language
eluded him. My mother, fifty-one, was a registered nurse
trained in England and passed the nursing board exams. She
soon began working at a local hospital.

In August we celebrated my eighteenth birthday. My
mother made my favorite Persian dish, *adas polo,* with plump

raisins, dates, lentils, and chicken tucked into cinnamon-scented rice. I had been known to eat an entire pot all by myself, so she had made an extra pot just for me and another one for our guests. Slowly we had been stocking our pantry with turmeric, cumin, saffron, cinnamon, allspice, dried fruit, lentils, fava beans, and basmati rice. In Iran, I had climbed onto the kitchen counter to look at my mother's cooking spices, opening them one by one, taking in their prickly scent. Now, it reassured me to see them lined up again like stepping-stones across a vast ocean. Rose petals and orange rind dried on our windowsills. Feta cheese and shelled walnuts with piles of fresh mint, tarragon, and basil accompanied our meals again. Without making a fuss, my mother helped me shed those teenage pounds, curbing my desire for the slick, processed food that had seduced me. We swam fifty laps in the afternoons when she came home from work, stroking parallel on our sides so we could chat. If we lost count, she'd laugh and make us start all over. We went on long walks together. We ate real food. And each time one of us came across the familiar, we gasped: *Oh, look! Look! They have persimmons here,* incredulous that people left them to rot on their trees, where they hung like fall ornaments. If we could reach a few that hung over a fence, we brought them home for my father, who loved to eat them chilled for dessert, scooping out the ripe flesh like parfait.

My mother made quick friends with the greengrocers and butchers in the supermarkets. They were always happy to see her, to slice into a cantaloupe for her to taste, teach her the names of different cuts of meat, or make suggestions for the Fourth of July. She loved reading the recipes in the food section of the *Fresno Bee,* where she learned what America was eating. She attempted these recipes cautiously, not certain what the final result ought to taste like, but nevertheless trying those for oatmeal raisin cookies, noodle casseroles, and bread stuffing.

Our home smelled familiar again, of cardamom and mint, jasmine and rose water. California's bountiful Central Valley provided us with plenty of the ingredients, from figs to pomegranates, dates, grape leaves, oranges, and almonds, to cook Persian food. Best of all, we had someone to share it with. My aunt and uncle were newly arrived from Iran with stories of their own about what they had left behind.

The night of my birthday party I had reached for ice and spotted the Jamoca almond fudge ice cream cake from Baskin-Robbins in the freezer. And over by the window sat a big square box wrapped in blue and yellow paisley paper. My cousin Roya and I had gone for a swim in the apartment complex pool. How we giggled when some gangly boys asked for our phone numbers. We imagined our fathers' faces when they answered the phone and heard a male voice on the other end asking to speak to their daughter. Obviously these boys had never encountered the wrath of an Iranian father. My father had a surgeon's massive hands. I had seen them pick up a boy by his ears and throw him out of the house like a kitten—

just another clueless kid who had been enchanted by my sister and thought he could sit next to her on the sofa and sip
his 7-Up, maybe even reach for her hand, only to be airborne
a minute later. When it came to suitable young men for his
daughters, it was a losing battle; no prince, no doctor, no en-
gineer or lawyer, could find a way into his good graces. How
in God's name was I ever going to go on a date?

After we showered and joined the family, my father made
us virgin Bloody Marys, and again, with the word *virgin,* we
collapsed into giggles. They urged me to open my present. Despite my uneasiness about my parents' buying me a gift with
their limited resources, I couldn't wait to tear away the paisley
paper. My brave, beautiful mother had bought me a turntable
with her first paycheck.

She sat on the edge of the couch, beaming. She said I
needed it for college. How did she know? My cousin gave
me the Rolling Stones' *Some Girls* LP. That summer we had
danced wildly to "Shattered" every time it came on the radio.
Behind closed doors, we would jump, thrust, punch the air
with our fists, and sing the lyrics at the top of our voices. I
studied the album cover—those funny wigs—and it was all I
could do not to rush to my room and play the album over and
over again until I knew every word to every song. If the summer of 1980 had a sound track, it would be *Some Girls* for the
two young women on the brink of an American journey, and
Ted Koppel's *Nightline* for the folks who hadn't asked for the
journey but were nevertheless thrust into its turmoil.

A few weeks later, in my college dorm room, I unpacked my precious turntable and leaned my single album next to it. On the windowsill, I put a snapshot of my birthday party: two young girls with our dark chocolate tans, broad smiles, and eager eyes, the first generation of Iranian Americans, sitting between my parents, my father's brooding eyes next to my mother's fragile optimism.

My Mother's Bread Stuffing

It is not surprising that Thanksgiving was my mother's favorite American holiday. She carefully observed the preparations her friends and neighbors made, collecting recipes, and over the years created her own traditional feast.

Stuffing for a 12- to 15-pound turkey or 2 5-pound chickens

1 large yellow onion

5 stalks celery

3 carrots

7 tablespoons olive oil

4 tablespoons unsalted butter

2 to 3 cloves garlic, slivered

1 to 2 whole cloves

1 teaspoon allspice

Zest of 2 oranges

1½ cups dried apricots, slivered

1½ cups dried cranberries

6 ounces chicken livers

2 loaves slightly stale peasant bread, preferably not sourdough

½ cup toasted pine nuts

½ cup coarsely chopped sage

2 tablespoons red wine vinegar

2 cups chicken stock

Kosher salt and fresh-ground pepper to taste

1. Preheat the oven to 325°F.

2. Dice the onion, celery, and carrot uniformly. Heat 2 tablespoons of the oil and 1 tablespoon of the butter in a skillet and
   sauté the vegetables with the garlic until soft and translucent.
   Add the cloves and allspice, half the orange peel, and the
   apricots and cranberries, stir together, and cook 3 or 4 more
   minutes on low heat. Remove and cool in a wide bowl.

3. Separate the lobes of the chicken livers, trim the veins, and
   dice into ½-inch cubes. Season with salt and pepper. Heat
   1 tablespoon each of the oil and butter and sauté the chicken
   livers until firm, about 3 minutes. Remove from heat, allow to
   cool, and add to the vegetable-fruit mixture.

4. Cut the bread into bite-size chunks, discarding the top and
   bottom crust. Toss with the cooked liver and the vegetable-
   fruit mixture. Fold in the toasted pine nuts and ¼ cup
   chopped sage.

5. Drizzle with vinegar and chicken stock. Taste for seasoning,
   adding more salt or vinegar if the stuffing tastes bland, and
   enough chicken stock to keep it moist.

6. To stuff the cavity of a turkey or other fowl, season the cavity with salt and fresh-ground pepper and gently scoop the
   mixture to stuff the bird. You will have some left over to bake
   separately. Pile the remaining stuffing into a buttered baking
   dish and gently pat down for an even surface. Dot the top

with the remaining butter, cover the stuffing with foil, and bake 1 hour.

7. For a 15-pound stuffed turkey, season the outside generously with salt and fresh-ground pepper, the juice of 2 oranges, and the remaining olive oil. Tuck the remaining orange peel and chopped sage between the breast and the skin. Place on the middle rack of the oven and roast for 4 hours, basting frequently and covering with foil once the bird is a rich golden brown. Remove from the oven. Cover loosely with foil and allow to rest 30 minutes before carving.

Note: The chicken livers and pine nuts are optional. Any preferred dried fruit may also be added or substituted.

Persimmon Parfait

· ·

Our first autumn in California was marked by the discovery of familiar fruits like figs and persimmons. It was remarkable to see branches on our neighborhood trees bowing with the weight of these bright orange ornaments, and no one to pick them. Perhaps our neighbors had once bitten into an unripe persimmon and vowed never to go near one again. So if we could reach any that leaned over a fence, we picked them. You have to be patient with persimmons— they're ready when they're ready, and that's that. When my mother asked a neighbor why she didn't pick her fruit, she exclaimed, Why, Amy, I wouldn't know what to do with them! *So my mother took it upon herself to help harvest persimmons, and soon, quick-bread and cookie recipes flourished. But my father still preferred to eat them straight up.*

When my sister-in-law came for Thanksgiving one year, we gave her some persimmons to take home to Maryland. She called a few days later to find out when they would be ripe. We told her the best way to know is to ask her husband to hold a persimmon in one hand and her breast in the other. When the two feel the same, the persimmon is ripe.

Serves 6 to 8

4 very ripe Hachiya persimmons
¾ cup sugar
3 egg whites
½ cup sour cream
½ cup cream cheese
1 teaspoon vanilla
1½ cups heavy cream
1 cup crumbled gingersnaps

1. Place 6 glass ice cream bowls or one large 9-inch bowl in the freezer to chill.

2. With the tip of a paring knife, gently remove the persimmon cores, then peel the skin away to scoop the flesh out. Place in a food processor and pulse until the fruit is pureed. Transfer to a bowl and chill.

3. Place ½ cup of the sugar in a small saucepan with 3 tablespoons of water to dissolve over medium heat. While the sugar simmers, whisk the egg whites in the bowl of an electric mixer until they form soft peaks. If you're using a candy thermometer, cook the sugar to 230°F. Otherwise, to test the syrup, you can dip in a knife, and if it forms a ball on the tip, it's ready. With the mixer running, gently drizzle in the syrup and continue beating until the egg whites are stiff and glossy. Transfer to a bowl and chill.

4. In the bowl of an electric mixer, whisk together the sour cream, cream cheese, remaining sugar, and vanilla until smooth, slowly adding the heavy cream in a steady stream until soft peaks form.

5. Fold half the egg-white mixture into the persimmon puree with ¼ of the whipped cream. Fold the remaining whipped cream and egg-white mixture together.

6. In the chilled bowls, put a spoonful of plain parfait mixture, sprinkle a layer of gingersnaps, then add a dollop of persimmon mixture. Continue alternating plain and persimmon, sprinkling gingersnaps between each layer. Tap each glass gently on the counter to release the air pockets and settle the layers. Cover with plastic wrap and freeze for at least 3 hours in small bowls, or 6 hours if using a large bowl.

7. If you wish to unmold the parfait made in a large bowl, uncover and immerse in hot water for a few seconds, then invert onto a chilled plate. Otherwise, remove the bowls from the freezer 20 minutes before serving, sprinkle the tops with the remaining gingersnaps, and serve.

Note: The parfait can be made a day or two in advance. When you wish to serve it, allow a few extra minutes to temper the frozen cream.

Chapter 4

THE GREYHOUND BUS station in Santa Cruz was quiet on Friday afternoons. After my last class I would take the campus shuttle into town and walk to the station. Waiting with the few other passengers for the bus that would take me home for the weekend, I looked forward to that two-hour drive on Highway 17 through the Santa Cruz Mountains. From my window seat I gazed at lush mountains the likes of which I had never seen, taking in the dramatic wildness of the California landscape.

Back at the dorm, my friends were planning parties, pooling their money for beer and rum. They watched me, bewildered, as I left every Friday afternoon. I'd say good-bye to my roommate, who liked to roll a perfect joint on her lap, taking her time sealing the paper with cat licks, looking flushed before roaming into a reverie, her thoughts cartwheeling from her parents to her boyfriend to Catholic school. I'd say good-bye to Frank, a bright boy who found me as exotic as I found him—a bleached-blond, tall, and lanky native. He told me stories about San Diego, where he'd grown up, its surf culture, the *meanest* burritos, his mother tending to her marijuana plants like prize orchids, and the little brothers he missed so much. I'd say good-bye to the boys in the quad kicking Hacky Sacks and to the lingering scent of clove cigarettes, and the last thing I heard was Bob Marley drifting through the open windows of the dorm's fourth floor.

I couldn't have planned a better initiation into California culture. This campus with its panoramic ocean views, its thick redwood groves and wildflower meadows, was as untamed and quirky as its student body. It was slow, organic, sustainable, vegan, long before those words became our everyday vernacular. They made their own granola and ate their vegetables unpeeled and raw. They introduced me to trail mix and marveled that Persians ate a similar mixture of dried fruits and nuts, minus the shaved coconut, carob, and banana chips.

Down the hall lived a music major with kitchen privileges, who went down to the wharf once a week for fish heads and tails. She came back to make big, messy pots of fish chowder. I liked to watch her make this crazy soup, throwing in whole, unpeeled turnips, carrots, and potatoes, clawing the skin off onions with long fingernails and tossing them in, ripping handfuls of celery tops, bursting ripe tomatoes in her fists, and all the while quietly singing melancholy Joni Mitchell melodies, even though the occasion called for Wagner. I stared wide-eyed at the fish heads bobbing to the surface, which stared back at me with milky eyes. She hardly waited for a boil before dipping a mug to feed herself, then turned to me with a Cheshire grin to offer some. "No." I said. "Thank you, but I already ate dinner." I was lying, of course. I had declined the food plan to save my parents the extra expense, but I did have a job in the school cafeteria making sandwiches at lunch, and I was allowed to make one for myself on my break. I learned to tuck enough ingredients between two slices of bread to sustain me for the rest of the day. But really, I couldn't accept the wild soup because I had grown up in a hospital where soup was made with washed, trimmed, and cubed vegetables, and the fish heads were strained from the broth before serving. Much later, when I learned to make bouillabaisse, I remembered my college friend—her appetite and her enthusiasm—and I regretted not having accepted a bowl of her soup.

I was compelled to go home on weekends to keep my parents company and to make up for the two years we had been prematurely separated. Their love was close and available, and unlike my fellow freshmen, I was no longer eager to distance myself from my parents. Having already flown the nest once, I regretted my blind cockiness—carelessly leaving them when they had needed me most. In my freshman year, my parents had moved to the Bay Area to seek better job prospects for my mother and board-exam preparatory courses for my father. Every weekend, they met me at the Greyhound station in Palo

Alto. It was comforting to slide into the backseat of their baby blue Pontiac and smell my father's cologne, to talk about what my mother had made for dinner and whether we would watch *Jeopardy!* or *Columbo.* Unlike during my high school years, I didn't feel a need to embellish my college experience, answering their queries about my courses and my professors candidly, telling them about a twentieth-century art history class, how I was mesmerized by the distortions in the cubist paintings. I boasted that a term paper on the parallels between the blues and classical Persian music had received praise, but then I left out my harsh sentiments about the premed courses and the mental anguish I suffered in chemistry class.

By the next morning, I would find them at odds over their new beginnings, each coping with exile quite differently. While my mother worked to support our family, my father faced another long day at home, where he slipped further and further into resentment. How does a man who had spent a lifetime building and healing pass time in idleness? Vacillating between rage and longing, day after day, he watched his wife go to work, bring home a paycheck, pay the bills, talk to the landlord, answer the phone, mail their letters, go to the bank—everyday tasks he seemed incapable of. He made repeated tries, but the board exams proved to be his nemesis. Thus robbed of his profession, he lost his ardor. He couldn't help wondering what would have become of them if my mother had steered clear of politics. Could they have gone home, quietly resumed their practice, and salvaged their identity under the glare of Khomeini? Could he see his wife living passively among the injustices of a theocratic regime?

I was in fourth grade when I first became aware of my mother's restlessness. As she nursed at my father's side, the hospital became too small for her. Though they shared the desire to transform their country, each had a different approach. My father knew he could make fundamental changes by running a modern hospital, teaching family planning, offering prenatal care, pediatrics, and even marriage counseling. My mother's vision was more broad and expansive, yearning to change the status of women in her country. My father feared for her against the corrupt, unwavering system she would be facing. She didn't wish to defy or abandon him, but her willingness to work as a team in the insular world of the hospital diminished every day. Ultimately she had to walk away. Her resolve eclipsed his objections.

My mother took on any establishment that did not give women a voice, and that was essentially every institution. If her drive had not coincided with that of a monarch who wished to modernize Iran rapidly, she most certainly would have been chided and silenced. But instead, she found the support and the blessings of Queen Farah. My mother found that she had a knack for politics and diplomacy, and soon she was on the boards of various organizations, fighting for women's rights, becoming the director of Tehran's first nursing school.

In the early seventies, she ran for a seat in parliament, representing Baft, in the province of Kerman. Her mother's family had cultivated pistachio orchards in Kerman for decades and she felt a personal connection to the area. At the time, only three other women presided in the 270-member legislature. The night of the elections, we listened to the results on the radio at a friend's house. When the announcer read my mother's name, everyone but my father raised a glass to toast her victory. He sat solemnly in an armchair, nursing a whiskey soda, and stared out the window. He couldn't share the magnitude of her accomplishment, seeing only that her victory was the first indication that they were becoming unglued as partners. He felt betrayed by her decision to be affiliated with politics, cynical that her efforts would have staying power—a precursor to what would follow one day in exile.

Immediately after her victory, she had taken a bus to her district some four hundred miles from Tehran, arriving in the early morning hours at a village where she walked the dirt roads with an aide. The townspeople came out of their mud huts to peer at her. Children circled her and she opened her purse, only to find a box of colored pencils she had always carried around for me. She said she had felt foolish dispensing them, but they were all she had and the children were delighted. She was appalled to find a forgotten village with no infrastructure, no schools, no clean water, no electricity, and no clinics. In the months and years that followed, she fought single-handedly to build schools, roads, and clinics for her constituents. My mother became their saint, and they would rush to kiss her hands when she came to monitor the progress.

At home she was defiant in the face of my father's accusations of abandoning medicine for politics. He resented her travels, her maroon diplomatic passport with the gold seal, her sudden launch into a world of bureaucrats and politicians he suspected of corruption, and their association with her as mere posturing for the Shah. To him, medicine had been their glue and their faith. But my mother had not turned her back on medicine. She saw her position as a means to an end. To open a clinic where doctors and nurses would stay, you had to build a road, provide running water, and build a school for their children. She saw the big picture; she recognized this remarkable era for women not just in Iran, but in India, where she met with Indira Gandhi, and in Israel, with Golda Meir, who was at the time the world's third female prime minister. My mother knew that, despite my father's objections, she had to stay the course.

By the time my sisters left for college in America, I had become accustomed to a different routine. I was a latchkey kid, coming home from school to find a note next to a pot on the stove with heating instructions for our dinner. My after-school snack of bread and jam was laid out on the kitchen table with a tin of instant cocoa and a mug. I missed our quiet afternoons together, but her sweet notes with an occasional doodle kept me company. I would keep watch by the window until I heard the sound of her wheels in the driveway, then rush back to my desk and pretend to be doing the homework I had finished earlier. Once in a while, she would be home when the school bus dropped me off at the corner. I was beside myself just seeing her green Peykan, a sedan manufactured in Iran, parked in our driveway. For the rest of the afternoon I would follow her around like a puppy, not letting her out of my sight. I couldn't stop talking, and to keep her engaged, I would embellish my stories with dramatic twists and turns. She would listen patiently, and at the first break in my monologue, she would pull a box out of her bag. A specialty of her district that she knew I loved was soft cakes with a date filling and a prayer stenciled on top with cinnamon. Maybe I was a fool to forgive her absence in exchange for a box of cookies, but I loved nothing more than to sit at the kitchen table while she made us a pot of tea, nibbling on date cakes and telling her about my day.

As the intensity of my mother's work increased, our family meals became tense, often ending with an outburst—my father pushing his chair away from the table, the harsh scrape of the legs wearing a groove into the tile floor. What followed were heavy footsteps to the bedroom, a door slamming, then weeks of moody silence where I became the vessel between them. No ship has carried a heavier burden than the child who bears messages between quarreling parents who refer to each other as *your father* and *your mother,* canceling any prior connection they may have had.

During these endless periods of cold war, my father would experiment in the kitchen, making his own meals as further rebuke to my mother. He would come home with a chicken, head and feet intact, throw it in a pot that was barely big enough, cover it with water, throw in a handful of dried plums, crank up the heat, and march away. Not long after, the smell of burning metal and chicken fat would seep under my bedroom door, where I would be keeping to myself, lest I be called upon to deliver a message. I would hear his footsteps rushing to the kitchen, the scalding lid he had picked up with bare hands crashing to the floor like cymbals, and the murmured expletives. I felt sad for him—too stubborn, too proud, too righteous—and would slowly get up, tiptoe to the kitchen, and ask him if I could make him an egg. Once in a while, when the chicken didn't burn, he would eat it standing up, right out of the pot, always leaving it, charred or not, on the counter for my mother to clean up. I would try to get to it before she saw it, knowing it would make her furious. Once, I even took a taste from a batch that had not burned but had nearly caramelized. It was delicious. The plums had given it just the right lift of sweet and sour, coating the chicken, which melted in my mouth in a gamy mixture of tangy, salty, sweet, and silky confit.

The long periods of silence would finally end with my father's coming home one day cradling an enormous bouquet of white lilies. The origin of their argument was tucked away in an overfilled grudge box, and the tedious cold shoulder would at last relent to a soft kiss. I knew, however, that another blowout was never far off. Later, I would observe other families' squabbles and feel relieved that ours was not the only family that nursed grievances, glad that the Persian predisposition to cherish a grudge was not exclusive to our family.

After they came to California, the tension between my parents escalated. As an antidote to her husband's resignation, my mother hurried to learn about the customs of her adopted country, nudging us along, giddy over the liberties that were now ours, too. Cutting out political cartoons from the *San Francisco Chronicle* that poked fun at Carter or Reagan, she would exclaim, *Imagine!* Studying the cartoons was also her way of tuning in to the American sense of humor so she could share a laugh. *I've got to know what's funny about that!* She chuckled over *Peanuts* and *Dennis the Menace,* cutting them out to put on the refrigerator door. At the hospital, she asked to be called Amy, a no-nonsense name, to spare her colleagues and patients the struggle to pronounce her Persian name, Atefeh. I imagine if they had known her name meant "compassion," they would have insisted on using it.

She chided fellow expatriates who wallowed in their loss, who criticized Americans, who at every turn looked for someone to blame for their misfortune, from Carter to the mailman who didn't have a letter from home. She refused to share their cynicism, and they did not share her bravado or her fierce self-reliance. There was no refrain in her zeal—she despised the clerics for destroying her country and felt indebted to the country that had offered her family refuge. There was no denying prerevolution corruption or abuse of power by the former regime, but she knew that the mullahs' brutality in the name of Islam far surpassed that of the Shah's secret police, that they would suppress women, gag them under their wretched veils, deny them equal rights, and put children, their softest target, in the line of fire in an ideological war.

At the same time, she was painfully aware that she would never again walk in the courtyard of her youth, lay flowers on her parents' gravestones, see her beloved Caspian Sea or the snowcapped Mount Damavand. She would no longer revel in the scent and preparations for Noruz, the Persian new year, which coincides with the first day of spring. Gone was the heady perfume of hyacinth, which lingered in the air for weeks before the holiday, as essential as the scent of pine in December. Plates of sprouting wheat would not line her windowsill. On the last Tuesday of the year, her children would not hold hands and leap over tumbleweed bonfires to dispel last year's maladies and draw from the fire's healthy glow. My grandparents would not be expecting us in our brand-new frocks and patent leather shoes, holding out our palms for shiny gold coins that we tucked into drawstring velvet pouches while staring longingly at the carefully arranged towers of delicate chickpea cookies and pyramids of baklava drizzled with rose water on my grandmother's coffee table. The first day of spring—could my mother let it come and go without recognition? Noruz is an intrinsic Iranian treasure. War, revolution, sanctions, jihad, fanaticism, will all take turns ripping a country apart, but Noruz prevails no matter where you're washed ashore, as do the food, the song, the poetry, and the art that heal any torn nation. People stagger, but they pick up a tattered thread and wind it back onto a spool.

The fervor with which my mother tackled the hard work of building a new home in a new land left her little time for lamenting the loss of her homeland, the carpet her father had had woven for her wedding, or her china and silver. Only occasionally, with a frustrated sigh, would she pull open a cabinet in search of a platter or a serving spoon to discover that it had been left behind in a kitchen drawer in Tehran. She would quickly recover and make a joke: *I hope the mullah's wife is enjoying serving her rice with my spoon.*

My father did not find her jokes amusing. It pained him that his beloved hospital, the scrubbed walls and surgical instruments, were contaminated by a flock of religious zealots who would lay waste to the very structures they would so desperately need after the war, when Iraq sent thousands of "martyrs" home without their limbs. He lamented the loss of his hospital as one would regret abandoning a relative in desperate times. He would recall its gardens and the north-facing balconies that lit up the patients' rooms. I imagine in his dreams he would walk the corridors and make his rounds, only to find the rooms empty. He could not see the upside of their exile, so while my mother chose to marvel at the miracle of America and its unbounded hopefulness, my father paced their small quarters and listened for Ted Koppel to bring him better news.

Braised Chicken with Persian Plums

. . . .

My father made this dish for himself when he had argued with my mother. Thus the memory of this dish is bittersweet. He would often burn it, the chicken charred and stuck to the bottom of the pan with the plums like a sad pile of coals. When it was caramelized, just before burning, it was delicious.

Serves 4

4 whole free-range chicken legs

3 tablespoons olive oil

1 large yellow onion, peeled and diced

1 tablespoon honey

1 teaspoon cinnamon

2 whole cloves

Juice and grated zest of 1 lemon

2 cups water or chicken broth

1½ cups pitted dried Persian plums or prunes

Kosher salt and fresh-ground pepper

1. Preheat the oven to 350°F.

2. Season the chicken legs well on both sides with salt and pepper. In a cast-iron skillet or a dutch oven over medium heat, brown the chicken, skin side down, in 1 tablespoon of olive oil. Briefly turn the chicken legs to brown on the other side as well. Remove the chicken legs and arrange them in an

ovenproof dish. Discard the fat, and in the same skillet, sauté the onion in 2 tablespoons of olive oil until soft and translucent. Add the honey, cinnamon, cloves, lemon peel, lemon juice, and broth. Bring to a boil, then turn down the heat and simmer for 20 minutes. Add the plums or prunes and check the seasoning, adding more salt or lemon juice according to your taste.

3. Carefully pour the broth with the plums over the chicken legs. Cover and braise in the oven for 1 hour. Remove the chicken pieces and plums, arranging them on a platter and covering them with foil to keep warm. Simmer the remaining broth until the sauce coats the back of a spoon. Spoon over the chicken and serve with soft polenta, couscous, or saffron rice.

Cinnamon Date Bars

....

*My mother used to bring me a box of soft, chewy date cakes from
her trips to Kerman when she visited her constituency. I instantly
forgave her long absences when she presented me with this specialty
of her region. Their closest relative is the Fig Newton—a happy discovery I made during my first year in America. It was only a matter
of time before I would attempt to duplicate them in my kitchen.*

*Experiment with your favorite combinations of dried fruit—such
as raisins, figs, and apricots—and nuts to make your own variation.*

Makes about 3 dozen

DOUGH

7 ounces (1¾ sticks) unsalted butter, cubed

½ cup sugar

1 egg

1 egg yolk

1 teaspoon vanilla

2½ cups flour

¼ teaspoon salt

1 egg, beaten, for brushing the dough

DATE FILLING

2 cups finely chopped dates

½ cup brown sugar

1 cup water

1 teaspoon cinnamon

TOPPING

¼ cup powdered sugar

1 teaspoon cinnamon

1. To make the dough, cream the butter and sugar in a mixing bowl until pale, about 2 minutes. Add the egg, egg yolk, and vanilla, separately, mixing well after each addition.

2. Add the flour and salt to the butter mixture and mix just until the dough comes together.

3. Turn the dough out onto a floured work surface and roll into a ball. Wrap in plastic and chill for 1 hour, or overnight if you like.

4. To make the filling, combine the dates, brown sugar, and water in a saucepan and cook over low heat about 8 to 10 minutes, until the mixture boils and thickens. Stir in the cinnamon.

5. Remove from heat and set aside to cool completely.

6. Preheat the oven to 350°F.

7. To assemble the bars, prepare a baking sheet lined with parchment paper. Remove the dough from the refrigerator and cut in half. Keep one half cool.

8. On a well-floured surface, roll half the dough into a rectangle about 14 inches long and 10 inches wide, and about ¼ inch thick. This dough is crumbly, so use your fingers to patch it if you need to. Roll the dough up onto the rolling pin and then unroll it on your baking sheet. Brush the surface with the beaten egg. Spread the date filling evenly down the center and out, allowing ¼ inch on the edges for sealing.

9. Roll the remaining dough into the same-size rectangle. Roll it up onto the rolling pin and unroll it directly over the dates. Press gently to seal. Trim the edges and brush the top with the beaten egg. Using a fork, lightly poke the top layer of the dough to make vents. Refrigerate 20 minutes.

10. Sift together the powdered sugar and cinnamon over the date bar before placing in the oven.

11. Bake 15 to 20 minutes, until golden brown. Remove from the oven and cool on the baking sheet. Slice into 2-inch bars.

Chapter 5

SUNDAY AFTERNOONS FOUND me waving good-bye to my parents from the smeared window of a Greyhound bus headed back to Santa Cruz. My mother would tuck dried fruit and nuts, chocolate bars, oranges, and a jar of jam into my backpack, so each time I reached for a book or my pencil case, I came up with a snack.

In the early evening lull of the dorm, I stepped softly into my room, where my roommate and I often left the door open, encouraging friends to drop by. *Hey, I'm back!* My roommate would greet me affectionately, bubbling over with stories of weekend hoopla that varied little from week to week: *Guess what? Michelle dumped Gary. She thinks she might be gay.* She munched gratefully on the snacks from home that I lined up before her. Frank would stroll in with a happy-to-see-you grin, sometimes bearing a gift: *Hey, I found this at Logos. You should really have it.* I would open the slim paper bag to find the Beatles' *White Album*, *The Doors*, *The Best of Van Morrison*, or Billie Holiday's *Lady in Autumn*.

You should really have it. He was diligent in his efforts to expand my repertoire, traveling the enormous distance between us with music, trying to translate himself while I held on to my otherness as a defense against losing something recognizable to me, to my family, to friends from home. What I learned from his music was essential. Billie Holiday's "Trav'lin' Light" broke through to me, her voice and the lyrics convincing me that this song was written for us, that we were not so different, that we were moved by the same words. And slowly I learned to trust these friendships that strengthened my still-fragile connection to this new country.

I was happy to creep back into my orderly college life. Beyond campus lay chaos—hostages at the embassy, Carter, Khomeini, Reagan, and the budding stereotype of the Iranian terrorist. On campus these elements were put in perspective, organized and explained within the parameters of history. The anti-Shah rallies, the Reagan protests, all were a reminder of the freedom that was now *mine, too.* But the upheaval I witnessed from afar happened before my political consciousness had taken shape. I was just barely beginning to discern the powers that trigger events and affect our lives.

When I was a child, my awareness of current events was initiated at my grandfather's house, where he welcomed us for lunch on Thursday afternoons. Inside, his house was dark, but the atmosphere was warm and smelled of sweet tobacco.

He liked to sit at his desk with his pipe and read the paper cover to cover, then solve the crossword puzzle with one hand around the slim waist of a glass of tea. Once the puzzle was complete, he folded the paper neatly along its creases, then handed it to me and sent me downstairs to a windowless room stacked from floor to ceiling with newspapers going as far back as my mother's birth. I glanced at this history of Iran on brittle, yellowed paper tied neatly in bundles, peeking at the headlines but never pulling on the strings that held them. *Kayhan* was the largest daily newspaper in the country, but even if I had read a story, it would have been a censored version of the truth. The paper was not allowed to print any criticism of the Shah, or any opposing political views within the country or abroad. Despite its liberal editorial staff, it was still heavily monitored and censored by the Information Ministry. I would not have learned anything about the dissident clerics or the disenfranchised left-wing "radicals" to give me a context for the revolution that would one day overturn our lives. I did not understand that we paid for political stability through repression. My grandfather knew this; he was better at reading between the lines, and he kept those newspapers as evidence of everything that was left unsaid. Leaving the day's paper behind, I wondered, *Why does he keep all those newspapers? What does all this have to do with now? It smells funny down here.* And, *What's for lunch?* I raced back upstairs to recite the multiplication table, or a poem he had taught me the week before, as a prerequisite to lunch.

Though I didn't participate in campus politics, this was a time when Iranian students had to take sides. We were obliged to explain the news and sift through the rhetoric and propaganda of the revolution for our professors and fellow students. Fearing the other Iranian students, not knowing whose side they were on, I became adept at telling my story in a matter-of-fact way, as if recounting the plight of another family. On campus I could engage in a dialogue that was increasingly difficult elsewhere, worried what my identity might provoke in a casual conversation at the post office. *Persian* quickly replaced *Iranian*. Where *Iran* was dark and threatening, *Persia* recalled glory, carpets, and cats.

> *Where are you from?*
> *Persia.*
> *This food is delicious. What is it?*
> *Persian.*
> *What is the origin of your name?*
> *Persian.*

Few people questioned where Persia was, not wishing to divulge their sketchy knowledge of history and geography. *Where are you from?* was a dreaded question. I felt that where I was from, where I'd grown up, where I called home, didn't matter. The point was that we had to leave.

The advantage of being from an ambiguous place is that one can spin tales worthy of Scheherazade. My college friends would sit cross-legged on the floor of my room, like preschoolers begging for a story from the exotic land of Persia. I amazed my audience (and myself) with tales of riding camels to school and never having seen a television set, a washing machine, or a hamburger. A favorite ongoing fib was about my camel Delilah, whom I rode to school every day:

Where did you keep her?
Why, in the stables, where else?

I had to avert my eyes when I explained that when the Revolutionary Guards came for my family and we were gone, they lined up our camels Czar Nicholas–style and shot them instead. I was astonished that they believed me.

Although I still often felt like an observer, sent to collect data on the natives' behavior, I was nevertheless beginning to feel I was a part of something. Walking through the redwood groves to my classes, I thought, *Yes, I, too, can stroll through campus holding hands with my boyfriend.* I was hoping my alienness would eventually become less interesting. Shuttling back and forth to the UC Berkeley campus to use the library or just wander down Telegraph Avenue, I became enamored of the diversity I found there, feeling a kinship with the parade of characters. It seemed that even if I were to sprout horns and a tail, no one would look twice. Browsing Moe's and Shakespeare and Company, I pulled books with penciled notes in the margins from the labyrinth of shelves, charmed to know that something I might have missed had happened in a passage. I loved finding handwritten inscriptions and the close, musty smell inside the pages. I lingered in coffee shops, with their makeshift sofas and chairs, the scent of roasted beans and incense clinging to my sweater like souvenirs on the slow bus home. I loved Sproul Plaza and the students of all political, religious, and social orientations who sat at their tables, earnest behind their movements, handing me free brochures. I didn't even know what *activism* meant. I only knew that I could partake in something that did not exist in my country: free speech. Reluctant to leave the one place that was beginning to assert itself, I also sought the anonymity Berkeley offered, so it wasn't long before I transferred. To please my father, I declared a premed major, with no intention of registering for any relevant courses, unless you make a connection between medicine and The History of French Cinema, or The Enlightenment and Eighteenth-Century French Literature. I continued to correspond with Frank. He, too, had left to continue his studies in England. Subsequent boyfriends did not measure up to his generous nature or his curiosity for the unfamiliar. Shallow in their worldview, they would not take someone like me home to meet Mom and Dad. Besides, who was I kidding? My father would have strangled them all, shallow or otherwise.

A part-time job in a coffee shop got me back in the kitchen, putting in as many hours as I could and carrying a full course load. I took so much pleasure in serving the stream of students who waited patiently for me to toast their bagels and gazed longingly at the strawberries I spooned onto their waffles. Our connection was uncomplicated—I could rely on their hunger and my ability to fulfill their need. It brought me back to the early cooking lessons my mother had given me in Iran, and to the school where I was first introduced to American food. The idea of *making things,* the alchemy of putting things together, had really taken root in me as a child. In my mother's kitchen, where pots of fluffy saffron rice, their lids wrapped in towels to capture the steam, sat on the stove, I watched her peel and salt eggplants, dice tomatoes, and brown a lamb shank with onions to make an aromatic stew scented with allspice and preserved lemons. I witnessed not only the transformation of these simple ingredients but its effect on people. My mother cooked because it made her happy, and when you sat at her table, you shared her happiness.

Back in Iran, my mother enrolled us in an English-speaking international school from elementary through high school. She had experimented with French schools and despised their medieval approach to education. At Jeanne d'Arc, run by Catholic nuns who punished my sister with a stick for giggling in the hallway, she had had a standoff with the mother superior: *Do French children not laugh, Sister?* she had hissed. Determined that her children be bilingual, she bought us English books, read *Peter Rabbit, The Wind in the Willows,* and *The Secret Garden* at bedtime, and sang "I'm a Little Teapot." The principal at our new school was a kindhearted American man. His wife was our music teacher, who taught us how to read notes and play the recorder. Neither of them had any intention of hitting us, no matter how much mischief we stirred. Instead, they let the vice principal, a short lady built like a tank, bawl us out. It was best to be invisible when she walked the hallways, her small head swiveling on her boxy frame, looking for the ringleaders. But she wasn't cruel, punishing children didn't give her pleasure, and if our parents heard we had been reprimanded, they knew we probably deserved it.

It was at school that I first became aware of the different smells at lunchtime. Whereas in my home, steaming rice signaled a midday meal, at school I smelled hot dogs for the first time, their delicious porky aroma luring me to the line outside the kiosk. I brought a lunch box, but oh, how I envied the children with lunch money who bought lunch from Madame's kiosk. The kiosk was a makeshift cabana where Madame, a grandmotherly Armenian lady with silver hair tucked under a net, and bright blue eyes behind wire-rimmed glasses, served hot dishes from a two-burner stove. I could smell her sloppy joes at eleven o'clock, during math, and my mind would wander for the next hour, my stomach counting the minutes with bold rumbling.

At noon I followed the kids over to the kiosk, their hands playing with the change in their pockets. I found a bench nearby so I could watch them while I ate my lunch. Madame ladled her homemade meat sauce onto soft buns and handed them through a tiny window. She kept soda bottles on ice and would open them with a bottle opener she kept tied to her apron. Madame made a simple cocoa pound cake and a spice cake, both lightly dusted with powdered sugar. How I longed for that pound cake. I would think about it all day, and when I couldn't stand it any longer, my best friend, Neda, would help me scrounge together some coins so we could buy a slice to share crumb by crumb. Later, much later, I would teach myself to make that cake, but it never tasted as good as it did in the school yard with my best friend.

Bake sales were equally enchanting. American moms brought brownies and chocolate chip cookies and carrot cake. I circled their tables, clutching a coin purse, reading the labels and pronouncing their delicious syllables quietly to myself, unable to decide. When I first bit into a brownie, I wanted desperately to decipher it. I wondered in what divine kitchen these recipes were invented. By what intuition had a pair of hands melted chocolate and butter and folded them into eggs with sifted flour? Did all these blessed fair children eat these squares of chewy cake with shiny, crackling surfaces after school every day while I ate bread and jam?

Recently, while gnawing on the end of a Twizzler, a friend asked me, *What kind of candies did you grow up with?* I paused before I said, *Roasted beets, sour green plums, furry green almonds, and salt-roasted corn on the cob.* Our snacks often came from street vendors we passed on our way home from school. In winter you could get a wedge of red beet that had been slowly roasting under coals and had caramelized. The vendor handed it to you warm, wrapped in newspaper, and you peeled away the charred skin, which left hennalike stains on your fingertips. In spring we looked for green almonds, which cost us a nickel for a dozen or so. They, too, came in newspaper cones with coarse salt, and a dozen was never enough. We ate the *gojeh,* sour green plums, by the pound and suffered the consequences. In the summer you found vendors with little charcoal grills on the side of the road, where they fanned their coals and yelled, *Balali,* while yellow ears of corn blackened on their grills. It may have been the only time I saw my father eat from *the outside,* fearful as he was of any food prepared outside the jurisdiction of a trustworthy home kitchen. Nevertheless, street food was our treat. My only candy was the lollipop I learned to make at home by caramelizing sugar in a pot and letting it harden on a spoon.

My mother never seemed concerned that I preferred stringing beans with her at the kitchen table to playing outside. I attempted to decode the flavors and textures that bewitched me, conducting experiments that often failed. But my mother indulged me, never minding the waste or the mess in the aftermath of disaster, but firm about my responsibility to clean it up. I relished these opportunities the way a child who practices magic tricks becomes convinced of his ability to transform a skeptical audience. I began every project with the bold premise that it was going to be delicious. In the space between the stove, the sink, and the refrigerator, I felt uninhibited and able to summon combinations with ease. I overmixed flour, eggs, and milk for pancake batter, I scalded milk for custard and ran to the pot when the foam had already pooled on the range, I rolled dough and it stuck to the counter. Enjoying my infrequent successes, my mother never complained about the lack of freezer space when I squeezed limes and dissolved sugar cubes, then froze the juice in glasses with a spoon to make Popsicles, or froze sweet, milky Nescafé to make what she called coffee ice cream.

AFTER GRADUATING FROM college, my sisters, in their desire to help my parents, quickly began working and married their college sweethearts—stalwart, brilliant American boys who brought the best of America to our family. My mother loved to cook Persian food for them, dazzling them with steaming platters of braised beef stew and jeweled saffron rice. Later she would delight in sewing her granddaughters' Gypsy skirts and tiaras for Halloween and hiding Easter eggs—a fresh embrace of new culture through them. My father, a tough nut to crack when it came to suitable men for his daughters, didn't hesitate to remark, *They could have done better . . . After all, we invested in their education,* and so on. Nevertheless, he was glad he was no longer outnumbered by women in the family. Finally there were men he could sit with, who called him Dr. Bijan and enjoyed a glass of scotch, and sweet granddaughters to peel pistachios for and bounce on his knee.

Although I grew up in a culture where food was cherished, this same culture did not esteem the culinary arts as a viable career choice for a university graduate. One weekend at home, I dropped the bombshell: I was changing my course of study from premed to French, with the intention of attending cooking school after graduation. My father's reaction was explosive; he refused to speak to me for months. The idea of his daughter becoming a *cook* was preposterous. *Cooks are domestics,* he would spit out. Cooking was something women learned to do from their mothers and grandmothers, a chore they repeated day after day for their husbands and their children. Restaurant cookery was for the uneducated. He hollered accusations that flourished alongside favorite banishments: *You are someone else's child!* My mother's response was dry, with a here-we-go weariness that pinched her pretty mouth. Something passed over her face like a cloud over the sun. I later understood this brief absence of light in her expression to imply her aversion to judgment. She believed a parent's job was to provide love and security without staking any claims on a child's future, that children owned their dreams, their mishaps, their triumphs, and their failures.

After the big announcement, my trips home became less frequent, leaving my mother to bear the brunt of my father's wrath. When she spoke plainly—*Her life is her business*—he accused her of complicity, implying that the hours I spent in her kitchen were part of a deliberate scheme to disappoint him. Now unreachable to me, he could not see that I was just following my calling as he once had, that I, too, could not fathom doing anything else with my hands. My mother prepared his favorite dishes as peace offerings—duck and pomegranate stew, grape leaf dolmas, smoked whitefish with dill and saffron rice, veal osso buco with extra marrow bones—all to no avail. She stood by me, never once questioning my decision, urging me to apply to cooking schools in France, offering to pay my tuition by taking on the higher-salaried graveyard shift at the hospital where she worked as a registered nurse. By graduation day I held a one-way ticket to Paris and a room to rent in the fifteenth arrondissement.

Sweet and Sour Grape Leaf Dolmas with Jeweled Rice

. . . .

Going for a walk with my mother was part exercise, part foraging, like an outing with a child. She rarely came back from her morning march through the neighborhood empty handed, unclenching her fists to reveal a bouquet of sage, tiny red plums, or a stack of nasturtium leaves. The plums would make two tablespoons of jam, the sage was tied with twine and hung to dry, and she saved the leaves for making her dolmas. Tender and peppery like watercress, nasturtium leaves were a fine alternative to the more tangy grape leaves. She served the dolmas garnished with nasturtium flower petals, like small presents.

Makes 35 to 40 dolmas

1 1-pound jar preserved, drained grape leaves
1½ cups lentils, preferably tiny French or flat green
1 whole clove
1 bay leaf
2 medium yellow onions
2 carrots
2 stalks celery
6 tablespoons olive oil
2 cups basmati rice
2 teaspoons cinnamon

½ teaspoon turmeric
½ teaspoon saffron (optional)
1 cup dried currants
4 cups chicken stock
1 tablespoon orange or tangerine rind
1 cup pine nuts, toasted lightly
Kosher salt and fresh-ground pepper
1 lemon

1. To remove the excess salt from the grape leaves, soak them in warm water for 30 minutes. Drain and rinse with cold water, then strain and pat dry with paper towels. If fresh leaves, such as nasturtium or butter lettuce, are available, select the largest ones and plunge a few at a time into boiling water for 1 minute to soften them, then lay flat on paper towels to remove excess water.

2. Rinse the lentils, then drain well. In a large saucepan, cook the lentils in 3 cups of water with the clove, the bay leaf, 1 peeled onion, 1 stalk of celery, and 1 carrot. Bring to a boil, skimming any scum that may rise to the surface, then simmer gently for 30 to 40 minutes, uncovered, adding more water as the last of each batch is absorbed, until the lentils are tender, with just enough cooking liquid to keep them moist. Season to taste with salt. Drizzle with 2 tablespoons of olive oil and set aside to cool to room temperature.

3. Dice the remaining onion, celery, and carrot and sauté over medium heat in 2 tablespoons of olive oil until soft and translucent. Add the rice, cinnamon, turmeric, saffron (reserving a pinch for later), and currants and toss well with the vegetables. Add 3 teaspoons of salt and 4 cups of chicken stock or water. Bring to a soft boil, cover, and cook the rice over low heat for 20 minutes. Allow to cool and transfer to a large bowl.

4. Blanch the orange or tangerine rind in boiling water for 30 seconds, strain, and dry on a paper towel.

5. In the large bowl, with a wooden spoon or spatula, gently toss the rice, lentils, citrus rind, and pine nuts. Season to taste with salt and pepper.

6. Preheat the oven to 325°F.

7. On a cutting board, lay 4 or 5 leaves side by side, vein side up (if the leaves are small, you can overlap 2 leaves). Place 1 heaping tablespoon of filling in the center of each leaf. Fold the stem over the filling, then fold the side flaps toward the center and roll up like a fat cigar. Continue until you have used up your filling.

8. Place the dolmas tightly next to one another in a buttered ovenproof dish. Dissolve a pinch of saffron in ½ cup warm water with 2 tablespoons olive oil and the juice of 1 lemon. Brush the top of the dolmas with this mixture. Sprinkle with

salt and fresh-ground pepper. Press a piece of wax paper gently over the dolmas to keep them moist and prevent them from unraveling. Cover with foil and place in the oven for 2 hours, until tender.

9. Remove from the oven and arrange on a platter with fresh herbs, such as tarragon, mint, and basil, or edible flowers. These are delicious served warm or at room temperature.

Madame's Cocoa Pound Cake

. . . .

*Madame, the lady who ran the lunch kiosk at my school in Iran,
made two simple cakes every day, spice and cocoa. She displayed
them under a cake dome, lightly dusted with powdered sugar, and
sold them for the equivalent of thirty cents a slice—a fortune to me,
and a rare treat.*

*I made a lot of pound cake before I came up with one that
resembled Madame's, but in my fond childhood memories, hers
still tastes better.*

*At Christmastime I make dozens of these cocoa pound cakes to
give to family and friends. This year, my son walked into the kitchen
as I was lining them up to wrap in cellophane and raffia.* Will any
of those *ever* be for us? *he asked, sighing. I set one on a plate with
a knife and made us two mugs of hot chocolate, and we sat down
to eat cake together.* Maman, *you don't always have to give them
away,* he reminded me.

Yields 1 9-inch Bundt cake

1 cup all-purpose flour
½ teaspoon baking powder
½ teaspoon baking soda
½ teaspoon salt
¾ cup unsweetened cocoa powder
6 ounces (1½ sticks) softened unsalted butter
1½ cups sugar

1 teaspoon vanilla extract

3 large eggs, at room temperature

¾ cup buttermilk, at room temperature

1. Butter a 9-inch Bundt pan.

2. Preheat the oven to 350°F.

3. Sift together the flour, baking powder, baking soda, salt, and cocoa powder.

4. In the bowl of an electric mixer with the paddle attachment, cream together the butter and sugar until light and fluffy, approximately 2 minutes. Add the vanilla extract. Beat in the eggs, one at a time, mixing well after each addition and scraping down the sides of the bowl.

5. Fold in the dry ingredients alternately with the buttermilk, mixing well after each addition.

6. Spread the batter evenly into the Bundt pan. Bake on the center rack for approximately 35 to 40 minutes, until a toothpick inserted in the center comes out clean.

7. Remove from the oven and allow to cool for 10 minutes before unmolding onto a wire rack to cool.

8. To serve, place on a cake plate and drizzle with chocolate glaze (see following recipe) or simply sprinkle with confectioners' sugar.

Chocolate Glaze

¾ cup heavy whipping cream
6 ounces dark chocolate, chopped

In a heavy-bottomed saucepan, scald the cream. Remove from
heat and whisk in the chocolate until the glaze is smooth and
glossy. Drizzle over cake.

Chapter 6

ALTHOUGH A TRUCE was called, the relationship with my
father remained strained after my abandonment of medicine.
He became more distant as rage, anxiety, and depression ate
through his body. Hearing the news that a brain drain had left
hospitals and clinics in Iran in dire shape, he saw an opportunity to go back. Much as America held promise for his family,
for him, it was the end of the road. He did not want to reinvent himself, negotiating daily between East and West. The
lush lawns bordered with perennials, the outdoor grills and
backyard swimming pools, the reliable postmen and friendly
bank tellers, the easy attire of belted khaki shorts and bright
polo shirts, going sockless in any weather, were another man's
comfort and would never be his. He loved nothing more than
medicine. Faced with the prospect of a safe and tidy life in a
California suburb, or the gritty, uncertain one in Tehran, he
chose the latter. Back in Iran, he was known. He had healed

mothers and babies, schoolteachers and shopkeepers, and they all noticed him when he walked down the street, bought melons from one of their stands, or stopped to muss the hair of their children. No one knew him in California. Here he was *Mister;* there he would always be *Doktor.*

In the seven years that had gone by, the hospital was occupied by various squatters, or as they preferred to be called, "revolutionary committees," but my father still carried the key to his clinic on his key chain. The authorities, having lost interest in his wife's whereabouts, renewed my father's Iranian passport, and at the first opportunity he flew home, took a taxi to his old office, turned a key, and walked in as if he had never left. Tehran's streets had been renamed to celebrate the revolution and its martyrs, so his clinic was now on Palestine Avenue, instead of avenue Kakh or Palace Avenue. What did he care what they called it, as long as he could get back to work? Word of his return spread quickly. Before long, patients knocked on his door, at first just to confirm that it was really Doktor Bijan, then returning with genuine ailments and gifts, bearing baskets of fruit, candy, and preserves. And when they found out he was alone, staying in the clinic, and sleeping on a cot, they brought him their homemade stews. I imagine my father slept well on that cot, content to have his work, speed-writing prescriptions only a pharmacist could decipher. His letters to my mother were mostly illegible, but exuberant. Unlike the community of specialists in America, my father knew his patients; he had been to their houses, met their spouses and kids, done everything for them from delivering their babies to removing gallstones. He began making frequent trips back, staying three to six months at a time, resurrecting what was left of his practice and his identity.

In reconnecting with friends, he pieced together a mosaic of his former life, discovering that the patterns we followed had altered little, that desire to come together in familiar places remained intact. Families we used to picnic with, or spend summers with on the Caspian shore, were now swept apart by the forces of revolution, but the remaining members continued to gather for weekend lunches, often inviting my father to come along.

Those patterns, synchronized to the seasons, had defined our lives. Fridays were our Sundays, and during the school year, my parents, who worked a rigorous six-day week, were ready for a day off. I could hear Friday mornings before shuffling to the kitchen. My father would be standing in his pajama bottoms with his back to me, squeezing fresh orange juice and listening to a Friday morning variety show on a Zenith radio he'd bought from an American family moving home. His voice joined the announcer's in a private tête-à-tête; he would sing and laugh at his jokes as they kept each other company before we wandered in for breakfast. He filled five little juice glasses one by one and held a glass under each of our noses, demanding, *Bottoms up!* In her mauve satin robe, my mother fried eggs and tomatoes in a black skillet, which she brought to the table with a dish towel wrapped around the handle. Fridays smelled different and sounded different, and the kitchen was filled with light and music until it was time to go on our regular outing. By late morning, we packed the car and drove to Niavaran, just north of Tehran, to the weekend house of my parents' friends. It was a simple villa with a sprawling tiered garden, where every weekend, the same group of doctors and their families would gather for an elaborate potluck lunch, a volleyball game, and garden siestas under the willow trees. They called themselves the Hal Club, which meant that they got together to *hal*—to seek rapturous delight and inspiration from nature. Often after their siestas, the grown-ups would be sprawled around on blankets in a circle on the lawn and someone would read Hafez or play a recent recording of the Persian blues or, best of all, sing. All the while, clear little glasses of tea were served from the samovar with sugar cubes, dates, and white mulberries. A friendly game of volleyball would follow on the sandpit at the far end of the garden, and on fall afternoons, there would be a long hike, with the women linking arms and the men clasping their hands behind their backs, engaged in discussions about real estate or politics. This was the only day of the week when I saw my parents relaxed, laughing out loud and playful, yet all the same I dreaded these long get-togethers, where I felt severed from my parents, who socialized and played volleyball with the grown-ups, forcing me into a circle of kids I didn't want to play with. Before leaving our house in the morning, I'd nag my mother about how long we'd have to stay at the party as she stacked Pyrex dishes of homemade stews, pot roast, and salads in the trunk of our car.

I sulked all day while the other children played tag and hide-and-seek. I was shy and preferred to be unnoticed, hiding behind my book, held two inches from my face. The grown-ups didn't interfere with the children's games or attempt to resolve disputes. A skinned knee, crusty with grit and blood, would be tended to later at home. A timid child would not be fussed over and coaxed into play. My parents were not yet aware that I needed glasses; my reticence to mention my blurred vision sentenced me to inhabit an interior world. I made it to fourth grade through guesswork and memorization—walking up to the chalkboard during recess to trace words with my fingertips and commit them to memory. If I had joined the other children's games, I could have run into a wall or failed to catch the ball and would have had to face their mockery. When I finally did get glasses, thick as saucers, it was a private epiphany, the crispness of it all—the chalkboard, the blades of grass, individual leaves. But it was too late to break out of the self-imposed exile I had already established with this group of children. In fourth grade, I would "blossom" only to the extent that an awkward child with square, gold-rimmed wire glasses could, and school was no longer a hazy mass of bodies with expressions I couldn't read—*Ah, so that girl is smiling at me after all! I could never tell if she liked me or not.*

In hindsight I think the Hal Club was a brilliant idea,

these bohemian physicians, sitting in a lazy circle on the grass, smoking their pipes, playing backgammon, reading poetry, and refueling before starting another week. Naturally all this bonhomie would come to a screeching halt if there happened to be a soccer match broadcast on television. This same group of renaissance men and women would huddle in a small sitting room in front of a black-and-white RCA, one doctor permanently assigned to adjust the rabbit ears while the others screamed and threw punches into the air. Finally, at dusk, they would reluctantly gather their dishes, my mother wrapping the remains of her pot roast for sandwiches. The buffet was never cleared until the very end, since everyone frequently had seconds and thirds as the day wore on. I skipped happily to the car ahead of everyone. We always arrived home in time to watch *The Fugitive,* dubbed in Farsi. Now here was a character I felt a kinship with. I was cautioned not to sit too close to the screen—*You'll ruin your eyes*—but my eyes were already ruined, and I liked the gray, grainy outlines of Barry Morse's face. My mother sat behind me, peeling oranges and arranging them on a plate we passed around with a saltshaker, as another Friday came to a close.

In the summer, we drove north to the Caspian Sea with a caravan of families. The long road to Ramsar was treacherous. I sat between my sisters in the backseat of my father's butter yellow Mercedes-Benz and watched the road curve, zigzag, and narrow, praying that I wouldn't throw up. I was always relieved when we pulled over to a grassy patch to eat lunch.

My father would cool bottles of 7-Up and Canada Dry in a shallow stream, and my mother would fold back the wax paper from chicken sandwiches and hand them to us. The day before, as she prepared for our trip, I had watched her poach the chicken with carrots, cloves, and leeks. She would let me gnaw on a few bones as she pulled warm, tender meat off the bird. I stood by and watched her fold chopped pickles, home-made mayonnaise, and fresh-ground pepper with the chicken pieces before spreading it on loaves of bread and cutting them into triangles. Sitting on our picnic blanket with her knees tucked under her cotton skirt, she would say, *I can smell the sea. Can you smell the sea, children?* But the shore was still many kilometers away. Back in the car she would distract us, pointing out the mountains that hugged the road. They were a soft yellow with specks of brown, like the inside of the currant cardamom cupcakes that I loved.

When the mountains gave way to the dark green rice fields, dotted red with women in traditional bright floral skirts, my father would roll down his window and take a long, deep breath. The sea was so close now you could feel the salt on your skin. In the afternoon light, the women sparkled like red bells, their backs curved, their arms extended over the crops, and my father would hum, softly at first, then joyfully, a native song his mother sung for him when he was a boy growing up here by the Caspian. It was a springtime song, beckoning a flower to bloom. A sing-along would follow, my father always amazed by my oldest sister's voice, as if he were hearing it for the first time. *She sings like a nightingale!* Inevitably there would be some discussion about voice lessons, which would be forgotten the instant we got our first glimpse of the water.

Our seaside vacations varied little from year to year. The children grew taller, marking the passage of time with new interests; one summer the girls still joined their younger siblings in a water fight, the next they asked you to rub olive oil on their backs as they lay flat on their bellies in moody silence, aloof to the boys who continued to wrestle with their fathers, hurling one another down on the hot sand. Fathers continued to wade in, holding the hand of a toddler who just last August had napped in a bassinet in the shade of a striped umbrella, and mothers offered great wedges of watermelon and handfuls of pistachios roasted with sea salt while remarking on new age-defying creams.

My father seized these days to eat the dishes of his childhood. He bought fish threaded on string from local fishermen, and fat fava beans, fresh eggs with bright yellow yolks, and roosters from nearby farmers. He waved and gave chewing gum from his dashboard to children who clustered around his car. His accent would slowly revert to that of the region, especially when he talked to the locals, and we giggled like crazy trying to mimic him. He wasn't forthcoming about his past. His father had passed away, leaving his mother to raise her five children with little means, and he had worked hard to break away and make his life far from his provincial upbringing, settling my grandmother in the hospital with us until she died when I was five. Proud of the man he had become, as if life had only begun when he was a medical student, he allowed me only glimpses of his youth through his obvious delight at being by the Caspian, foraging for the flavors of his childhood, chuckling with the fishermen. I tried to imagine him as a young boy kicking a ball on the sand, and it baffled me that a person could grow up by the sea and not learn to swim, but my mother explained that he had been too busy, taking care of his younger siblings and studying, to go to the beach: *Darling, the sea was just there; it wasn't exotic, as it is to us coming from the city.* But I held on to a belief that people who grew up by the water were playful by nature. My father may have had to shoulder responsibilities I couldn't fathom in my coddled life, but there was no doubt that the salt air drew out his humor, and he grew expansive. Everyone came to anticipate his juvenile pranks, like setting up my uncle to give swimming lessons to a pretty young woman on the far side of the beach, only to run back and get my aunt to come see what her husband was up to, then standing back to watch my aunt berate my poor uncle in front of a growing audience, my father laughing his head off like a schoolboy just warming up for more mischief.

After spending the day on the beach, we would walk back to the simple villas we shared with the other families. We sat at long picnic-style tables and ate whole grilled fish drizzled with bitter oranges from the local orchards, or fava bean omelets with flat parsley, or rooster stew, while our fathers fought over the coveted rooster's comb, considered a delicacy. As summer wore on, our mothers wrapped their hair in floral scarves to hide the beginnings of graying roots. My mother made marmalade, peeling the oranges we had picked for her, filling the villa with fragrant citrus, her fingertips still bearing the tangy scent when she stroked my forehead at bedtime.

On his return trips to Iran, my father did his best to participate in the old string of dinners and get-togethers, but after a while he stopped going. He couldn't summon the enthusiasm for returning to our old haunts. He was no longer the jovial companion who loved to play practical jokes, like tying everybody's shoelaces together while they were napping, or putting their hats in the freezer when it was snowing. It was all he could do to keep his clinic open and see his patients, sleeping on the cot in the corner of his office, cooking his old chicken and plums on a two-burner tabletop range. He would return home to my mother in California, frail and tired to the bone.

When I reconnect with my childhood friends, dispersed though we may be, we tenderly reminisce about our mothers and fathers and their affection for us, holding one another's hands to walk back in time. We keep our shared memories in deep storage until we see one another, and then we dust them off, showcasing them one by one, like precious antiques.

Remember the time you shot yourself in the groin?
Yeah, and your dad yelled at me for a half hour before he took the bullet out!

Remember how you'd throw up on the drive to the
    mountains?
It was one sniff of your evil egg salad sandwich that made me
    do it!

Remember when we drank your dad's vodka?
Sure, and we filled the bottle with water.
As if he wouldn't notice!

We collapse laughing over one another while our spouses sit back and grin politely. If it weren't for these friends, I would worry that I had imagined all those picnics, all those small, only-funny-to-us, you-had-to-be-there incidents that reveal who we are and where we came from. Without them, these memories grow milky with time, and my ability to sort through them becomes myopic. What remains fixed are the warm scents and flavors of childhood, like the cherry syrup that flavored our summer drinks, the sour fruit leather we shared in the backseat of the car, the sharp scent of sumac on grilled skewers of kebab. We may not agree on whose car we were in, or where we stopped for kebab, but the essentials are clear and true, understood by nobody but my family, my sisters, my cousins and childhood friends.

My Mother's Pot Roast

. . . .

My mother often made this pot roast (although she called it roast beef) for our Friday potluck lunches with friends. She varied the vegetables—root vegetables in the winter, peas in the spring—but toward the end she always added potatoes, which were cooked until tender and coated with the meat juices.

Serves 4 to 6

4 pounds top rump of beef, tied in a compact shape
4 cloves garlic, peeled and halved
6 tablespoons olive oil
1 medium onion
4 carrots
4 celery stalks
4 medium tomatoes
1 tablespoon tomato paste
1 bay leaf
4 strips orange peel, 2 inches long
4 sprigs thyme
2 cups red wine
1 cup beef or chicken stock
2 pounds Yukon Gold creamer or fingerling potatoes, peeled
½ pound brown cremini mushrooms
Kosher salt and fresh-ground pepper

1. With the tip of a sharp knife, make small incisions in your
   roast and insert the garlic cloves. Rub the roast with salt,
   fresh-ground pepper, and 2 tablespoons of olive oil. Cover and
   marinate your roast overnight if possible. The next day, remove
   the roast from the refrigerator 1 hour before cooking so it will
   be at room temperature.

2. Preheat the oven to 450°F.

3. Place the roast on a rack in a deep roasting pan and put in
   the center of the oven. After 20 minutes, when the roast has
   browned evenly, remove from the oven. Lower the heat to
   350°F. Remove the rack from underneath the roast. At this
   point the meat can remain in the roasting pan or be transferred to a dutch oven.

4. Peel and chop the onion, carrots, and celery into ½-inch
   pieces. Skin the tomatoes by plunging them into boiling water
   for a few seconds. Cut them in half horizontally, scoop out the
   seeds, and chop the tomatoes. In a skillet, over medium heat,
   sauté the onions, carrots, and celery in 3 tablespoons of olive
   oil just until they are tender. Add the tomatoes, tomato paste,
   bay leaf, orange peel, and thyme. Stir to coat the vegetables.
   Add the red wine and bring to a light boil. Add the stock and
   simmer over low heat for 10 minutes. Pour over and around
   the meat.

5. Cover the pan with foil or, if using a dutch oven, a well-fitting
   lid. Put in the oven and cook for 1½ hours.

6. Wash, drain, and halve the potatoes and mushrooms. Toss with 1 tablespoon of olive oil, salt, and fresh-ground pepper. Remove the pan from the oven and fold the potatoes and mushrooms in around the meat. Cover and continue cooking another 1½ hours.

7. To serve, slice the roast into ¼-inch slices and arrange on a platter with the potatoes. Remove the thyme, bay leaf, and orange peel and pour the sauce with the remaining vegetables into a saucepan to bring to a boil before spooning around the roast.

Note: Any leftover meat can be saved for sandwiches, or shredded and tossed with fresh noodles and the remaining gravy.

Fava Bean Omelet

A variation of this dish, baqala ghatoq, *hails from northern Iran near the Caspian Sea, where my father grew up with four brothers and sisters. With chickens pecking in the yard, my grandmother could make this delicious and economical meal for her family with the freshest eggs, their yolks bright as saffron. My mother learned how to make it from her mother-in-law, but she made it her own with the addition of fresh herbs.*

In the traditional recipe, the fava beans are cooked longer, until they are nearly pureed, and the eggs are cracked and fried directly over the beans. In my version, I cook the beans just until tender, then add a pinch of sugar, to caramelize the shallots with the beans, and fold them into an omelet. I'm certain you will find a variation, too, and whether it's scrambling the eggs or adding juicy bacon, croutons, or smoked salmon, it will be delicious as long as you have fresh eggs and young, tender fava beans. With a glass of dry white wine, it's a royal meal.

Serves 4

2 pounds whole fresh fava beans
2 medium shallots, diced
2 cloves garlic, minced
2 tablespoons olive oil
A pinch of sugar
8 large eggs

3 tablespoons unsalted butter
Kosher salt and fresh-ground pepper
½ tablespoon fresh Italian parsley, chopped
½ tablespoon fresh tarragon, chopped

1. Shell the fava beans by removing them from their padded pods.

2. Bring 2 quarts of salted water to a boil and blanch the beans for 1 minute to ease peeling the second skin. Rinse with cold water and strain. Gently peel away the outer skin (they should pop out easily). Discard any beans that are yellowing. Peeled, they yield a little over 1 cup.

3. In a skillet, brown the shallots and garlic in olive oil. Fold in the fava beans, allowing them to soften, then gently break them up with a wooden spoon and toss with a pinch of sugar. Remove from heat and set aside.

4. Crack the eggs and whisk with 1 teaspoon of salt just until the yolks and whites are combined.

5. To make the omelet, set your pan on low heat and allow the bottom and sides to heat thoroughly.

6. Once your pan is heated, turn the heat to medium, add the butter, and tilt the pan to coat the bottom and sides. When the butter begins to sizzle and foam, pour in the eggs and allow them to form and get puffy around the edges, then

scramble with a spatula and leave for a few seconds to form another edge. If the eggs begin to brown, lower your heat. Continue to scramble and set until the eggs are halfway done. Scatter the fava bean mixture and the herbs, tilting the pan to let the raw egg slide down to the hot surface of the pan. Season with salt and fresh-ground pepper. Continue to push the set eggs into the cooked mass. Tip your pan to push the omelet to the edge, and with your spatula, fold one end over itself. Repeat with the other end. Nudge any errant favas back into the folds.

7. Slide onto a warm platter and serve immediately.

Chapter 7

MY MOTHER FLEW with me to Paris, holding a return ticket for two weeks later. During the flight, she held my hand for comfort as I lamented the new relationship I was leaving behind. Here I was, finally on a flight that would deliver me to my dream, after my mother had endured two years of my father's wrath and worked double shifts to supplement her salary to pay for my cooking school, and I couldn't stop hot tears from rolling down my face. She gave me her white cotton handkerchief with pink roses embroidered along the edge without mentioning the doomed nature of the relationship— a girl who questioned faith, in love with a Jewish boy from a conservative family. There were no words of caution, not even a *Mind your heart,* the way she would've said, *Mind your step,* if I were walking to the edge of a cliff. She knew that her children would love whomever they chose, that their hearts would break, and that other than offering comfort, parents were powerless. It was clear to her I would dismiss her wariness as old-fashioned bunk: *Oh, Mommy, it's 1984!* As if that had anything to do with it. Ah, what young people don't know—what seemed to me full of possibilities, she saw for the dead end it was. But I had to learn such hard lessons on my own.

As we circled over Paris, she pointed out the Eiffel Tower and the Arc de Triomphe, which looked like toys on the grid surrounding the river Seine. It was a pearly white morning, and the captain's voice was reassuring as he deftly pushed through the clouds to land. I wiped away my tears with my mother's handkerchief—I could be in love *and* learn how to cook. The two were not mutually exclusive, and in fact, each longing could tend the other.

We boarded a shuttle bus to the city, and the driver quickly began a flirtatious exchange: *Ah, c'est super les sœurs qui voyagent ensemble! Ah, how nice to see sisters traveling together!* As I counted the change for our tickets, I was glad that my degree in French was not useless and I could participate in these harmless and necessary flirtations without becoming flustered. I replied, *En plus, elle est beaucoup plus belle, n'est-ce pas? And she's far more beautiful, isn't she?* After we'd taken our seats, my mother reached into her purse, broke off a piece from a chocolate bar, and popped it in my mouth: *Welcome to Paris, sweetheart!* I don't know whether it was hunger and fatigue, or the exhilaration of being with her on this adventure, but I had never tasted chocolate so good. That taste remains my first memory of Paris. To this day, when I travel to France, I always take the shuttle, and I always tear open a bar of chocolate and gaze out the window to spot the first red awning of a café with its rattan chairs scattered on the sidewalk. Then it feels as if I have come home.

We found my flat—a maid's room down the hallway from a three-bedroom apartment, where the tenants rented their housekeeper's quarters for extra income. My aunt Farah, who was living in exile in Paris, had secured this lovely little room for me. She had sneaked in before our arrival to open the big window overlooking the Seine and leave a neat stack of sheets and towels on a simple cot next to a bowl of purple grapes. I may have been lovesick, but the sight of those grapes on the white table, and the cool breeze blowing in from the river, made everything right. We put our bags down and rushed to see her. What a feast she had prepared for our arrival: pomegranate and duck stew, jeweled rice, and chocolate éclairs from Dalloyau for dessert. Everything in Paris tasted delicious, even the cup of coffee she brewed for me in her percolator with a lump of sugar stirred into it.

The next morning, with a great sense of urgency, my mother marched me to the market on the avenue de la Motte-Picquet, which runs along the underpass of a metro line, where in no time she filled our shopping cart with big heads of lettuce, cheese, eggs, flowers, and a chicken—its head and feet intact. She walked briskly through the stalls, as if she had always shopped in this market, chatting with the vendors, persuading them to select only the ripest peaches and most perfect clusters of grapes for her. I did my best to keep up with her as she pushed through the crowd, pulling a red and black tartan-print cart we had borrowed from my aunt for the day. This was my first field trip, and having grown tired of explaining to me that to learn a craft well, you must go to the source, my mother was enjoying the show-and-tell. We rarely argued, but in the months before my departure, I had debated that I didn't need to go to France for cooking school. After all, Berkeley was a food mecca, and why couldn't I learn by working in a renowned restaurant? It was the only time she persisted: *If you're going to do this, then do it right.* I now understood why she had brought me to the market on my first morning and why she had insisted on Paris. Markets and restaurants exist everywhere, but very few have the sensual appeal of a French still life. I had walked along only a few crooked streets, but already I felt as if I were inside a painting, a large canvas commissioned by a hungry gourmand with urgent desires: pheasants, cockles, mackerel, ceramic tubs of crème fraîche, slim green beans, and fat little golden pears in pyramids under the watchful eye of vendors prohibiting your touch. But I wondered what on earth she planned to do once we returned to my tiny flat, where the kitchen in the coat closet was never intended for anyone to make leek and potato soup or chicken fricassee on its two-burner stove.

For the next few nights we cooked and invited Aunt Farah and my mother's old friends from Iran. I made us coffee, and there, with the toasty smell enveloping my little room, they sat on the cot and told stories of their shattered lives. Poets, ministers, housewives, journalists, doctors—all disenfranchised citizens who had narrowly escaped the sweeping hand of the Revolutionary Guards prowling the streets and making random arrests. The men held the tired gaze of hopelessness, while the women looked defiant, their anger still palpable after six years. They blinked wildly, and tears welled up in their eyes at the mention of a sibling, a spouse, an aging parent, a friend, a colleague in hiding, on the run, imprisoned, dead, or simply left behind. Families were rarely intact, mothers and children having been sent abroad while fathers stayed to work and sustain the lifestyle their spouses were accustomed to. Those who joined their families spent their days brooding over lost fortunes while their resourceful wives consigned hand-knit sweaters to boutiques or became seamstresses who offered alterations, taking in hems and putting shoulder pads in old jackets to bring them up to date. Fiercely proud and acutely aware of perceptions, they kept up appearances. My mother understood their vulnerability, knowing all too well the thin line that existed between security and homelessness. Her friends translated displacement and despair into chronic aches she had no cure for, but she admired their resilience, the brave face they put on for their children, and how they kept an eye out for fellow expatriates, the husband who had lost his wife, or the daughter on her own for the first time, showing them how to make long-distance calls, accompanying them to the post office, bringing them home for meals.

They asked me curious questions about America: *Is it true that women go to the grocery store with curlers in their hair?* As if this infraction, above all, made it an intolerable place. How absurd this concern for style: *Who cares what they wear to the store when they can voice an opinion and not get thrown into jail?* My mother knew to brush off these comments: *Every time I leave our apartment to go to the store, my neighbors ask me why I'm all dressed up. Well, what should I wear? And you know I can't wear shoes without hose!* Her friends nodded. They couldn't imagine my father either, always dapper, going out for eggs in a jogging suit. Their queries revealed a unique Persian sensibility: *Aren't they quite gullible? No,* I answered, *they take things at face value.* It wasn't the first time I had heard American friendliness misconstrued as naïveté, a candid *Hi!* interpreted as oafish. They wondered how people could say, *Have a nice day,* and just go about their business, wheel their shopping carts, and walk their dogs, when there were places where children were sent to mine-filled battlefronts. On the other hand, Iranians are quite good at not saying what they mean, concealing their disapproval of everyone else with poetic euphemism, scrutiny veiled in praise: *Is that rich mahogany the natural color of your hair? Of course someone of your stature must drive the latest Mercedes-Benz, but we're very happy with our Camry. This carpet is very nice, looks antique, is it machine made?* These deprecatory remarks are essential to Iranians for survival in their society, which runs on the engine of ruse and conspiracy. Overt friendliness implies artlessness. Speaking in a circuitous manner, dodging a direct exchange, is considered cunning and clever. It was amusing to hear a fresh hybrid of Farsi emerge as Iranians assimilated into new cultures. An American friend described her outrage when early in her marriage, her Iranian husband told their dinner guests in Farsi, *This scanty meal was hardly worthy of you.* When he translated for her, she refused to speak to him for days. He quickly learned to tone it down: *My wife is learning to make Persian food. Please don't be afraid to try some.*

Perhaps my mother's friends were voicing a perception and hoping to be contradicted. It was foolish to hold their preconceptions against them. It was their way of finding out if there was a place for them where *they* wouldn't be judged, where they could hope for security, where everything they uttered would not be lost in translation. I called them all Auntie and Uncle. Aunt Farah was my closest and dearest aunt, though we had no connection by blood. It comforted my mother that my aunt would be an important presence after she left. She lived a block away and was generous, never meddlesome, and almost as fun to be with as my mother. She was too gay to commiserate with the community of expatriates who paced their cramped apartments chain-smoking and arguing with their spouses.

When my mother was preparing to leave, she drew a vivid contrast between the resolute life she was returning to in

America and the anguished state of her friends smoldering
in France: *I've had a lovely time, but I have to get back to work.*
There were colleagues and supervisors who expected to see
her, there were rent and bills to be paid and a daughter's tuition to be earned. We opened a bank account, into which she
deposited an allowance, and I was given a checkbook bigger
than my pocketbook, suggesting far more than the actual sum
in the account. I rode the shuttle back to the airport with her,
both of us somber this time as I squeezed her hand in mine.
Not one for drawn-out partings, she tucked her handkerchief
into my pocket and walked quickly to the gate.

Paris at any era, at any age, is glorious, but when one is
twenty-two and pursuing a career in cooking, it's extraordinary. I attended the Cordon Bleu in 1984, during its last year
under the direction of Madame Brassart, the same five-foot
lady who had made Julia Child miserable in 1949. At eighty,
she was still a formidable presence, appearing unannounced
to taste student's dishes and scowl at failed attempts.

Our mornings began with a quick review of the day's menu
with the portly Chef Simon. His round wire-rimmed glasses
would slide down his nose as he panted through the recipes. He then left us under the supervision of Chef Petroff, a
manic-depressive genius we adored. He never bothered to learn
our names but simply hollered our countries of origin: *Es-
pagne, Japon, Iran, Sénégal, va chercher un moulin! Hey, Spain,
Japan, Iran, Senegal, go get a food mill.* He was flirtatious in
a matter-of-fact, what-do-you-expect-from-a-Frenchman way.

Sliding behind women, he would sniff their necks, playing a guessing game of name that perfume: *Ah, Guerlain! Shalimar! J'ai été sûr! Ah, I knew you were wearing Guerlain's Shalimar!* He had owned a reputable boulangerie before the long hours, the oppressive daily production, and the sheer demand had driven him mad, forcing him to sell his business and turn to teaching. Fortunately for us, his passion had remained intact, so when he talked about a daube, his voice would boom against the heavy copper pots that lined the kitchen. When he taught pastry, his voice dropped to a near whisper as he kneaded a ball of dough, murmuring softly, *Touchez-la avec toute la tendresse, comme une jeune fille. Treat it tenderly like a young girl.* Sometimes I can still see his gnarly hands on the floured butcher-block table, showing me how to fold puff pastry for *palmier* cookies, generously letting sugar fall between his fingers like snow, and the perpetual murmur, *Voilà! Tu as compris, Iran? Tu as compris ou non? Ce n'est pas la cuisine arabe ça. Here, you see, Iran! Do you understand or not? This is not Arab cooking.* Even this racist barb didn't bother me. I knew he had never finished school. I knew he had apprenticed in the back of a bakery at fourteen. I knew he thought Iran, Iraq, Saudi Arabia, and the entire Middle East and North Africa were just one big Arab nation with an unrefined cuisine consisting primarily of sheep's testicles, but I forgave his ignorance because underneath this manic exterior was a good man who loved his work and taught us generously.

On his dark days, Chef Petroff would not look at us,

barking instructions and flying into a rage if we forgot to skim the stock or used the wrong knife to fillet the fish. Fearful and anxious, we tiptoed around him. On one of these gray Parisian days, a copper saucepan filled with a broken hollandaise sauce flew across the kitchen and hit my forehead. Through yellow glop and blood that oozed down my face, I saw his expression, savage with disgust, as he spat: *Iran! C'est la merde, ta sauce! Iran! Your sauce is shit!* I stood frozen in shock until someone took me to the washroom to clean up.

The next day I skipped class for the first time. I walked to the Champ-de-Mars, past the shops on the rue Saint-Dominique, and through the avenue de Suffren, where they piled the sidewalk bins with oysters as early as eight o'clock in the morning. I sat on a bench for hours, nursing a fantasy that Chef Petroff would see I was missing and come looking for me. But of course he did not. I made a decision that I would not speak to him ever again. I returned to school the next morning, and my determination held for the first hour. I succeeded in avoiding Chef Petroff until he called me over to watch him debone a duck, casually reminding me that duck galantine would be on my next exam, so I had better pay attention. He held the duck liver in his palm and joked about how he wished his liver looked so bright. I realized this was his apology. After all, I was there to learn to cook; how could I stay mad at a man who loved his craft, one who took my failed sauce as a personal insult? And that was the end of our *crise.*

The mornings were busy, with the entire class rushing

about preparing the three- or four-course menu of the day, classic French bourgeois dishes like *navarin d'agneau, salade landaise, lapin à la moutarde,* vichyssoise. By noon everything had to be ready, and the long table in the kitchen would be set for lunch with pitchers of watered-down Côtes-du-Rhône. Our lunches were festive. We teased one another over mishaps, shaving off the charred edges of a gratin—*The oven was too hot!*—and passing out spoons for a runny flan. How else would we have learned the difference between a correct beurre blanc and a broken sauce that puddled like an oil spill? The chefs never ate with the students, joking that we might poison them. They ate in the office, often a simple meal they prepared for themselves, like a *steak haché,* a hamburger patty with a fried egg on top.

After lunch, we cleaned up and went to a café on the corner of the rue Cler, where we would have coffee for one franc. This was a luxury for me. I had to decide between coffee and the loaf of bread I would buy on my way home for dinner. If my aunt had asked me to dinner, then I would enjoy a coffee and put two lumps of sugar in it. Unlike many of my classmates, who indulged in restaurant meals and weekend excursions to the country, I lived frugally, counting on lunch at school to sustain me.

Afternoon classes were demonstration courses, where Chef Simon would prepare dishes from his seemingly endless repertoire and we would observe and take notes. Some of my classmates skipped the afternoons, going sightseeing or lingering in a *salon de thé* over rich pastries and thick hot chocolate. Blowing off class was not an option for me, since it was clear to me that this was my future and I knew how much my mother had sacrificed so I could be there. My notebooks were filled with drawings and recipes that I copied onto index cards every evening. This solitary, rote exercise of rewriting, editing, and cataloging recipes was immensely gratifying, albeit obsessive. And being devoted to a boy far away, I couldn't accept dinner invitations from young men. Instead, I composed letters in Farsi, an increasingly difficult endeavor, since I was losing my vocabulary and my handwriting had begun to resemble a second grader's. Perhaps this was a foolish way to spend precious Parisian nights, but the writing satisfied my youthful longing.

Most evenings, on my way home I would stop to buy half a baguette, then head to the *fromagerie* for a wedge of cheese I had never tasted, and finally go to the produce stand for a single peach, or two figs, maybe a tomato. I lingered in front of bistros and watched the diners through the beveled-glass windows, framed like paintings. They ate noisily, joyfully, all elbows on narrow tables, engaged with their dinner. They waved their arms in the air and cradled glasses of red wine. They tied big, square napkins around their necks and swallowed oysters. Waiters like orchestra musicians in starched white shirts, black vests, and ankle-length aprons whisked plates away, gliding between tables balancing platters high above their heads, expertly opening and pouring bottles of wine. For me, watching them was as good as eating with them.

Home in my tiny kitchen, I improvised meals. I loved my room. I loved coming home, opening the curtains, putting on my slippers, and making dinner. I would make a pot of rice and chop a tomato over it; I would shred a potato and sauté it in butter and tuck a piece of cheese inside for a pancake. I set the table with cloth, silverware, and a napkin and ate ceremoniously, looking over my notes from the afternoon class. Sometimes I invited my classmates for dinner parties. When teaching yourself to cook in a closet, you learn that you can cook anywhere. On my two-burner range, with my postage-stamp sink and minirefrigerator, we composed meals from school that consisted of six ingredients or fewer and did not require an oven, although a few show-offs attempted stuffed partridges in aspic. We shared the cost, and we brought our own dinnerware. We forgave our mishaps and were happy to huddle on my bed, plates on our laps, watching the room light up every time the *bateaux-mouches* tour boats cruised by on the Seine.

The preoccupation with belonging that had plagued me in America seemed to peel away, and in its place I found myself at ease in Paris. As at my school in Iran, I was surrounded by students from all over the world with the same purpose of learning. Cooking and eating together, we enjoyed a kitchen camaraderie that I came to know well in the years to come.

Speaking French allowed me to communicate with our chefs, understand their jokes, and translate for my classmates the ones made at their expense. Most important, I was taken seriously, making it clear that I had no intention of cooking as a hobby.

And I made Paris my own. My small budget allowed me to walk the streets and its museum of food, always taking alternate routes with a dog-eared *plan de Paris* in my pocket. My mother had shown me how to read maps, her pink-polished fingernail tracing a river, pointing to a monument, teaching me to look for landmarks: *Never be afraid of getting lost.* I learned the city avenue by avenue, marking my way with bistros, bakeries, butchers, cheese shops, distinguishing the sharp smells and chatting with merchants in each neighborhood, falling in love with a city that was always preparing for a party. I enjoyed the brisk Parisian pace, keeping up with the men in blue work overalls who ducked into bars for a quick coffee and a smoke, the office guys with bright-colored blazers swinging schoolboy briefcases, the women in tailored coats with one hand resting on the bag worn across their shoulders and the other holding the mittened hand of a child who trotted to keep up, and ladies maneuvering shopping carts on their way to the market. I felt that I, too, could walk with them so purposefully.

On Sunday mornings I waited for a call from home, relieved that I no longer had to go to great lengths to convince my mother of my well-being. Being exactly where I belonged allowed me to speak frankly and contentedly. One Sunday's call brought news of my father, who would be stopping in Paris to see me on his way back from Iran. Not having had much contact with him since my arrival in Paris, I was anxious about being trapped with him in a small room, left alone to face his scorn.

Straw Potato and Muenster Galette

In my little room in Paris, I taught myself to cook low-cost, one-skillet meals on a two-burner range. I experimented a lot with this potato cake, substituting goat cheese, Gruyère, Roquefort, chives, or black olives. One of my favorite fillings, of which you need just a small amount, is the Alsation Muenster cheese, especially when studded with cumin seeds. As you slice through the crisp potatoes, an unexpected flavor and texture awaits. This potato cake makes a lovely light dinner with a green salad and an Alsation Riesling. For a more substantial meal, pair it with roast chicken, rabbit, or steak.

Serves 4

3 large Yukon Gold or russet potatoes
6 tablespoons butter, melted
3 tablespoons olive oil
Kosher salt and fresh-ground pepper
A pinch of grated nutmeg
2 ounces Muenster or preferred cheese, sliced ¼ inch thick

1. Wash and peel the potatoes. Shred them with a grater or a mandoline and immerse in cold water for 20 minutes. Strain and pat dry thoroughly with a dish towel.

2. In a nonstick 9-inch skillet over low heat, pour 2 tablespoons of melted butter, the olive oil, and ¾ of the potatoes. Tamp them down with a spatula and cook over medium heat for

8 to 10 minutes. Shake the pan to make sure the potato cake moves around freely and continue to press it down. Season with salt, fresh-ground pepper, and grated nutmeg.

3. Check the bottom by gently lifting one side up with a spatula. Lower the heat if it is browning too quickly. When it has turned golden brown, lay the cheese on top in a single layer. Pack the remaining shredded potatoes on top, pressing down again to make the galette as compact as possible.

4. Carefully flip the galette over, or slide onto a plate and invert the plate over the skillet, so the golden side is up.

5. Pat the cake down again and add the remaining butter around the edges. Continue cooking about 10 minutes, until the bottom is golden brown.

6. Slide onto a cutting board and dab with paper towels to drain the excess grease.

7. Cut into eighths. Sprinkle with salt and fresh-ground pepper. Serve immediately.

Roast Rabbit with Whole Grain Mustard and Rosemary

....

I had seen rabbit on enough chalkboard menus, as I made my way home from school every night, to yearn for a taste. I could never afford a meal at any of those bistros, but I could buy a rabbit and cook it at home, maybe even invite my classmates.

This dish taught me that you really need only two pots, a skillet and a saucepan, two sharp knives, a fork, and a spoon. I have been in enough gadget-happy kitchens, where there is no evidence of any actual cooking going on, to know you only need half of whatever you think you may need to equip your kitchen. That's what you learn from cooking in a closet.

Serves 4

1 rabbit, about 3 pounds, cut in 6 pieces
Kosher salt and fresh-ground pepper
½ cup olive oil
1 tablespoon coarsely chopped rosemary
3 strips bacon
3 cloves garlic, crushed
½ cup white wine
1½ cups chicken stock
3 tablespoons whole grain mustard
½ cup heavy cream

1. Cut up the rabbit, removing the hind legs first, then the forelegs. Cut the back loin in 2 pieces and trim the belly flaps. Refrigerate the belly flaps separately to use later. Marinate the rabbit pieces with salt and fresh-ground pepper, a drizzle of olive oil, and 2 teaspoons of the chopped rosemary. Cover and refrigerate for at least 6 hours, or overnight.

2. Preheat the oven to 350°F.

3. Slice the belly flaps and the bacon into 1-inch pieces.

4. Heat 1 tablespoon of oil in a large, oven-proof skillet over medium heat, sauté the bacon and belly flaps with the crushed cloves of garlic until golden, then transfer them to a plate. Mop up the rendered fat, leaving just enough to brown the rabbit pieces. Over medium heat, sauté the rabbit on both sides, adding the pieces to the plate with the bacon as they brown.

5. Deglaze the skillet with white wine, scraping the bottom of the pan to release the caramelized bits, and simmer 2 minutes. Add 1 cup of chicken stock and simmer 5 minutes.

6. Crowd the browned rabbit pieces back into the pan and tuck the bacon mixture in between.

7. Use a spatula or a spoon to spread a thin, even layer (⅛ inch) of whole grain mustard (about 2 tablespoons) along the back of the rabbit pieces. Sprinkle with remaining chopped rosemary.

8. Bring back to a simmer and cook until about 1 inch of stock remains in the skillet. Cover and place in the oven to cook for 1 hour, removing the cover during the last 10 to 15 minutes to brown the mustard coating.

9. Transfer the rabbit and bacon mixture from the skillet to a platter and cover loosely with foil to keep warm. Add the remaining ½ cup of stock to the cooking juices in the pan, simmering just to loosen the browned pieces on the bottom. Strain into a saucepan and bring to a simmer, skim, and add the cream. Swirl the sauce and whisk in 1 tablespoon of mustard, simmering just until the sauce coats the back of a spoon. Season with salt and pepper.

10. Drizzle the warm mustard sauce over the rabbit. Serve immediately.

Chapter 8

ON THE AFTERNOON before my father's arrival, I tidied
my room, made the bed for him with fresh sheets, and borrowed blankets and a mat from Aunt Farah for extra bedding.
Knowing he had not had a hot, home-cooked meal in three
months, I wanted to make him a nice dinner and show him
that I had learned something. With the few francs I had left
at the end of the month, I bought the ingredients for a ratatouille but realized I did not have enough for the eggplant. In
desperation, I pinched it from the grocer. In a swift intercep-
tion by the manager, I was caught. He listened as I told him
my pathetic story through anguished sobs. Being a kind man,
he allowed me to run home for my checkbook. Later that
night, my father praised the ratatouille, yet noted the resemblance of the dish to a common Persian eggplant dip. *So this
is what you've learned? Your grandmother could have taught
you this.* Still gripped with fear from my earlier encounter

with the grocer, and the threat of going to the gendarmerie, I couldn't meet my father's eyes. I had let him down again—a disappointment, like everything else in his life.

My father stayed for a week, and I was grateful to Aunt Farah for having us over most nights and inviting his peers for conversation, indulging them with whiskey sodas and salted pistachios. The feeling of apprehension was still there when we returned to my room and while I made his tea and boiled him an egg in the morning before going to school. It was there when, later in the day, I debated whether I should walk home to see him or sit in the café with my friends. My father and I receded into the corners of the room, eyeing each other like strangers, unable to simply say, *How about a walk by the river?*

In an incredible gesture of parting, he gave me a cookbook by a treasured author, Rosa Montazami, considered the Irma Rombauer of Iran. On the inside cover, in his best hand-writing, he had written: *For my daughter.* It meant that he was still capable of tenderness toward me. And this gift allowed me to consider his feelings; I was the daughter who ought to have been a son, following his father's path—Dr. Bijan's son, the *doktor,* not Dr. Bijan's daughter, the cook. It was not an unreasonable wish for a father, a wish he had harbored before I was even born and one I had thwarted with my first cry. Yet he continued to set himself up for disappointment. When I was a child, he would frequently call me to assist when he tackled a broken screen door, changed a bulb, checked his engine oil. I was to hold the funnel, or pass him nails or a screwdriver laid parallel on a tray like surgical instruments. Bent over his task, he knew without looking if I was about to chuck a bent nail: *Leave it. I'll straighten it out. Come hold this while I screw it in place.* It was like an arm-wrestling match I would never win. As simple as my part seemed, I managed to fumble, letting go of a latch just as he was reaching for his hammer, handing him a wrench when he'd asked for pliers. I tested his patience, hoping I would be dismissed, but he chose to overlook my ineptitude. His voice would gradually rise— *Listen, LISTEN! I said PLIERS!*—refusing to let me leave until the task was done. In Iran, I would never have dared to stray from his expectations and would have ended up a clod in a white coat. It was America's fault, really, for giving me a taste of liberty, of choice.

IN MY FINAL months in Paris, I prepared for the final exam, which would be judged by Madame Brassart. The chefs had forewarned us not to be fooled by Madame's age. Years might have softened her since the days when she mocked Americans and delayed Julia Child's exam to postpone her graduation, but her judgment remained swift and brutal. From time to time, she would lurk in the back of our classroom, gray hair pulled back in a neat bun, the slightest tremor in her chin suggesting a perpetual *non, non, non.* No one dared look up to meet those glassy eyes that roamed the kitchen and didn't miss a thing.

As the school prepared for its last days under her command—for she had sold the Cordon Bleu to the Cointreau empire—I saw my class as the end of an era. The new school would be moving to a different site with fancy modern equipment. The women would no longer be required to wear blue pin-striped frocks and tie their hair back with handkerchiefs, but they would have starched chef's coats and paper toques, a far more uncomfortable uniform. I was glad I had been part of the old school, with its damp walls, banged-up copper pots, whisks with missing wires, and dented ladles that generations of cooks had handled. All that would be stored away, and a chapter of French cuisine under the old guard would close. Chef Simon was retiring to the Loire, and Chef Petroff, I later learned, took his life the following year.

My final exam consisted of two parts: the preparation of duck *à l'orange* in front of a panel of chefs and Brassart, and a surprise assigned on the morning of the exam. My mother had come to Paris for my graduation, which would take place after the exam, provided I passed it. The week before the exam, my aunt Farah bought a duck every day from her neighborhood butcher, and I would prepare duck *à l'orange* while she and my mother chatted, drank tea, and played cards. Sometimes my aunt would set up a chair in her bathroom, wrap a towel around my mother's shoulders, and order her to sit down. Then she'd give her highlights, or put her hair up in a pretty chignon. I'd smile to myself, hearing their voices carry to the kitchen, their sudden shrieks of laughter like that of schoolgirls.

Every night, Aunt Farah would invite a few dinner guests, who would eat my duck dutifully. They'd ask polite questions about my future plans: *What, after all, is Dr. Bijan's daughter going to do now that she can cook duck?* After they left, the three of us would make another pot of tea and take the dish apart, my mother and my aunt giving me feedback while I washed the dishes. They both came to my final demonstration. As if at a recital, they sat in the audience with open smiles and nodded *bonjour* to everyone. A glance at their faces put me at ease. I could make duck *à l'orange* blindfolded.

The morning of the surprise assignment, I woke up before dawn to pore over my index cards one last time. While I made us café au lait, my mother dashed to the bakery for croissants. She walked with me to school that lovely June morning and we admired the chestnut blossoms on the trees. Spring had come late that year, and we were seeing Paris in her prettiest dress.

Upon my arrival, I was given an envelope with my exam handwritten by Chef Simon on notebook paper. I had two hours to make *pâte à choux* and then use the dough to make *éclairs au café, gougères au fromage,* and cream puffs for a *gâteau Saint-Honoré.* I tied on my apron, which my mother had washed and ironed the night before, and found in the pocket a little note from her, wishing me good luck. I turned on the ovens and gathered the ingredients, reciting the recipe I had memorized. I piped the first batch of éclairs so big that, once baked, they looked like toddlers' shoes. Started over. In the last forty-five minutes I was filling oval shells with coffee custard that was a little runny. When Chef Simon walked in promptly at eleven o'clock, I was more or less finished, quickly wiping up the little pools of custard that were oozing out of my éclairs. I was dismissed and the chefs gathered to taste and grade my efforts.

I learned that Madame Brassart had given my duck a 19 out of 20, remarking with a shaky voice that she was surprised I had not ruined the dish by making it too sweet, as Americans always tend to do with everything, *mon dieu!* I think it pained her to give that underhanded compliment, and Chef Petroff had a good time giving me the verdict, mimicking her quivering chin. The éclairs, despite the telltale puddles of custard beneath them, received a respectable 15, owing to the correct crispness and size of the shells (if they'd only known) and the flavor of the coffee custard, which was *assez bon,* good enough.

Before returning home, my mother took me to Printemps, a department store behind the Opéra, to buy a new dress. Spring itself paraded inside and bloomed on every rack. We each carried an armful of dresses to the fitting room and I tried on dozens before choosing one, a scoop-neck, belted jersey, pink with tiny white tulips. We shared a *croque-monsieur* and a lemon tart before going to Dehillerin, the quintessential cookware store, where I painstakingly selected five heavy copper saucepans, a boning knife, and assorted baking molds. We rode home on the metro, carrying my purchases wrapped in brown paper and tied with string. What pleasure to stroll together the next morning, me in my new dress, to be part of that Parisian splendor. I was seeing it all again as if for the first time: the patisserie windows with glistening rows of berry tarts, the delivery vans unloading crates of champagne, the elderly man in the café who winked at me over his coffee cup. Even the Eiffel Tower looked new when we turned a corner—there it was, magnificent and alone in the early light. We met Aunt Farah for one last coffee before catching the shuttle to Charles de Gaulle—this time an even quicker good-bye.

To celebrate graduation, a few of us planned a trip to the Loire Valley, shepherded by an American classmate who had been behind all of our occasional diversions: a side trip to sample ham at the charcuterie, pistachio macaroons at Trocadéro, leaving class early to go to a sandwich shop off the Champs-Élysées for all-you-can-eat *raclette*—that marvelous warm mountain cheese shaved onto your plate with pickled pearl onions, cornichons, and small boiled yellow potatoes. He never steered us wrong. He scouted these places while we were in afternoon classes and returned with persuasive arguments why we mustn't waste our time in a stuffy old classroom, how we could learn everything beyond the walls of the Cordon Bleu. So when he suggested a trip to the Loire, we were in, packing ourselves into a Renault 5 rental car so we could share the expenses. We visited châteaux and picnicked on the banks of the Loire, drinking Sancerre and eating Crottin de Chavignol goat cheese on baguettes with radishes, apricots, and thick slices of *saucisson*. We had dinner on the patio of a family-run restaurant, where I had squab for the first time, with a warm chanterelle salad. I almost wept when they wheeled in a magnificent cheese cart, laden with delicate domes, furry pyramids and cylinders, tiny buttons and bells of goat cheese with soft names: Chabichou, Sainte-Maure, Selles-sur-Cher, Charolais, Clochette, Cœur du Berry. Alas, my mother's foresight had been impeccable. I had caught a long-lasting fever.

Soon after graduation, I secured an apprenticeship at Fauchon, the tony patisserie on the place de la Madeleine. For weeks I waited for the pastry chef outside the employee entrance, offering my slim credentials until he finally let me into his kitchen. I was the only woman among nineteen boys, ranging in age from fifteen to eighteen, in a low-ceilinged basement kitchen under the supervision of a toothless head baker, Monsieur Jean. At five o'clock every morning, I ran downstairs to join the boys with tousled hair and bloodshot eyes on an assembly line where we folded croissants and *pain au chocolat,* or rolled brioche buns and secured their caps. For months, under the oppressive weight of flour that settled on my eyelids, in my ears, and on the bridge of my nose, I toiled in a Dickensian dwelling where hierarchy ranked me at the very bottom next to Abdul, a man from Senegal. In this kitchen I witnessed the horror of French racism, these unapologetic and entitled young men insulting a man who washed their pots and pans, cleaned and tended their ovens, and brought them fresh pitchers of hot coffee, offering sugar cubes from an old fluted bread mold. The cruel monkey jokes bounced off him as he stopped to give them a refill. Monsieur Jean hollered at him if the croissants were ever so slightly dark, ordering him to throw the entire tray away. I would shuffle across the flour-dusted floor to commiserate with him. Together we stared longingly at the pile of rejected croissants in the garbage bin. How I wanted to reach in to grab one and shove it in my mouth.

Subsisting on nothing but Abdul's strong coffee all morning, I was ravenous and grateful for the homey stews, soups, and casseroles the cafeteria madams would serve us at lunchtime. Monsieur Jean would go home at noon, having been there since three in the morning making dough. He lived with his wife outside Paris, where they proudly tended their rabbits, ducks, and geese. Monsieur Jean often told us stories about chasing the rabbits for their supper.

I rarely saw the executive pastry chef. He came in at nine o'clock and spent the morning with his top aides in the *laboratoire,* the oval office of the kitchen, constructing the elaborate cakes that would line the windows of Fauchon. In the 1980s you could not walk down the narrow sidewalk in front of the shop without groups of tourists asking to have their picture taken with the cakes. When people found out where I was apprenticing, they imagined I was behind those cake monuments, but I told them no, I was perfecting the continental breakfast.

On Fauchon's main floor, ladies in cream-colored frocks hurried behind the counter, taking orders from chic Parisians and indecisive tourists. They arranged the miniature fruit tarts and raspberry napoleons in signature pink boxes and trilled, *Avec ça? Anything else?* When they called on the intercom for backup pastries, the boys would parrot their high voices and hurl crude, tired jokes they had made up about the saleswomen. I gladly carried trays upstairs to get a peek at the shop and sniff the lovely perfumes of the customers with their Louis Vuitton handbags and Hermès scarves. The counter ladies were mostly kind to me, though they thought I was simple or crazy to stay in the basement with nineteen adolescent boys. But I approached my downstairs colleagues as an older sister would, and they left me alone, except for one skinny-hipped Pierre, who begged me for English lessons. He invited me to his parents' apartment for dinner and I came prepared with notebooks, sharpened pencils, and a box of chocolates for his mother. She made us roast chicken, rice pilaf, and a salad with whole tender leaves of butter lettuce in the kind of lemony Dijon vinaigrette only a Frenchwoman can make. Pierre had no intention of learning English. Instead he taught me an important *truc,* a trick. Linking his arm through mine, he showed me how to fold my lettuce into small, neat packages so as not to bruise the leaves I had been severing with a knife. I ought to have used the knife to fend off Pierre's roaming hand on my lap. I edged farther and farther away on my seat until he gave up and pouted. He had to find another English teacher. Given my unrequited devotion to the young man in California, I could not fathom romance with Pierre, and I had been naive in my judgment of both men. At least here, I could stand up and say thank you and good night to Pierre and his parents, but I had left a clumsy trace of long, passionate letters to the other that I could not retrieve: *Good-bye, now may I please have my half-eaten heart back?* I was thankful the next day when the boys largely ignored me, having pegged me as a prude.

The glimpse into the rough underbelly of a French kitchen did not deter me. It amused me that more than once I was asked if I planned to marry a baker to help him mind the shop. At twenty-four, I struck them as *vieille fille,* a spinsterish girl. For these young French cooks, this job, at Paris's most esteemed patisserie, was the pinnacle of their career. Few of them would have the means or the opportunity to strike out on their own, whereas I was just getting started—and on my way back to America.

Ratatouille with Black Olives and Fried Bread

··

It's impossible for me to make this dish without thinking of my father and how I almost went to jail preparing it for him. In the summer we can barely keep up with the abundance of zucchini from our garden, so I make big pots of ratatouille, browning each vegetable in batches before returning them all to the skillet and adding the tomatoes for a final quick toss. Whether served with croutons or as a side to grilled meats, or forgotten in the fridge for a few days, where the flavors just get better, it is a perfect summertime dish.

Serves 6

6 Japanese eggplants, chopped in ½-inch cubes, unpeeled
1 cup olive oil
1 large yellow onion, diced
3 cloves garlic, minced, and 1 whole clove
2 red or yellow bell peppers, chopped in ½-inch pieces
6 zucchini or any yellow squash, chopped in ½-inch pieces
¼ teaspoon saffron
2 to 3 sprigs thyme
6 medium tomatoes, peeled, seeded, and chopped
¼ cup black olives, *niçoise* or Kalamata,
    pitted and chopped coarsely
Kosher salt and fresh-ground pepper
1 loaf chewy sourdough *bâtard* or *ciabatta*

1. Preheat the oven to 400°F.

2. Toss the eggplant in a bowl with salt, pepper, and ¼ cup of olive oil. Transfer to a greased cookie sheet in an even layer. Bake approximately 15 to 20 minutes, until lightly browned and soft. Baking the eggplant allows you to use less oil.

3. In a large saucepan, heat about 3 tablespoons of olive oil and sauté the onions until they soften and glisten. Add the garlic and cook another 3 minutes. Add the peppers and season with salt and pepper, cooking over medium-high heat until they are tender and browned. Transfer to a baking sheet.

4. In the same saucepan, sauté the zucchini in 2 tablespoons of olive oil just until they begin to brown and soften. Season with salt and pepper.

5. Over medium heat, gently fold the peppers and onions and the eggplant into the zucchini. Add the saffron and thyme. Fold in the tomatoes and increase the heat to cook the vegetables together for another 5 to 10 minutes without stirring too much. The vegetables should not be immersed in a pool of their juices. Pour any excess liquid out and reduce it in another pot until thickened before pouring back over the ratatouille.

6. Transfer the ratatouille to a bowl and cool. Remove the sprigs of thyme. Fold in the chopped olives, drizzle with 2 tablespoons of olive oil, and adjust the seasonings if needed.

7. Rub the crust on the loaf of bread with a halved clove of garlic. Cut into ½-inch-thick slices, brush with olive oil, and brown both sides on a griddle, or bake in a preheated 400°F oven until golden brown.

8. Serve the ratatouille cold or at room temperature with fried bread, or fold into eggs for a delicious frittata.

Duck à l'Orange

....

*Graduation from the Cordon Bleu was twenty-five years ago, but I
still remember the confidence that came with learning how to cook
all the things that had until then mystified me. I knew how to fold
butter into dough for puff pastry, I could cube vegetables uniformly
and transform them into soup, I learned how to press goose livers
through a sieve to make pâté. And when I walked past a butcher
shop, I could buy a duck, take it home, and roast it. The weeks lead-
ing up to my final exam were like the movie* Groundhog Day: *every
afternoon I'd be trussing a duck at four o'clock, and the doorbell
would ring at seven o'clock—our dinner guests arriving to sample*
canard à l'orange.

*Don't let the fancy name stop you; it's no different from roasting
a chicken, but perhaps more festive. Use Seville oranges, if they're
available, for their exquisite tartness and aroma. I save the duck
livers and sauté them separately with a teaspoon of shallots and a
drizzle of red wine vinegar to mash up on croutons as an appetizer,
or toss in a salad with radicchio, orange slices, and crispy strips of
bacon for a quick, delicious dinner.*

Serves 4

1 duck (3 to 4 pounds), trimmings (neck, wing tips) reserved
Kosher salt and fresh-ground black pepper
3 oranges, scrubbed to remove the wax, 1 whole,
    2 for zest and juice

3 whole cloves

1 medium onion

2 medium carrots

2 celery stalks

3 tablespoons honey

1 lime, zest and juice

3 clementines, zest and juice

1 cup chicken stock

4 sprigs thyme

¼ cup cider vinegar

2 tablespoons butter

1. Preheat the oven to 450°F.

2. Remove the neck and the wing tips from the duck and reserve for later use. Season the duck generously, inside and out, with salt and pepper. Place 2 sprigs of thyme and 1 orange studded with 3 cloves in the cavity and truss. To truss, place the duck, breast side up, on a cutting board. Using kitchen twine and a trussing needle, poke through the upper part of the wings to secure them to the body. Then pass the needle in the opposite direction through the thighs. Tie the ends of the twine together and snip off the extra string. Trussing allows the duck to cook more evenly.

3. Place the duck on its side in a roasting pan and slide it into the oven. Roast for 10 minutes, then turn over onto its other side

to roast for another 10 minutes. Turn the duck on its back and roast for 10 more minutes.

4. While the duck is roasting, dice the onion, carrots, and celery into ½-inch cubes.

5. Remove the pan from the oven and surround the duck with the aromatic vegetables, neck, and wing tips. Turn the oven down to 400°F. Return the pan to the oven and continue roasting the duck for approximately 15 minutes per pound (therefore a 4-pound duck would roast for about 1 hour). Every 10 or 15 minutes, baste the duck and vegetables with the cooking juices to keep them moist, working quickly so as not to lose the oven heat.

6. Remove the duck from the oven and transfer to a platter. Cover loosely with foil and allow to rest a minimum of 25 minutes before carving. If you don't need the oven for anything else, turn it off and place the duck inside with the door ajar to keep it warm. It will continue to cook while it rests.

7. To make the sauce, discard the liquid fat in the pan and place the roasted trimmings and vegetables on medium heat to brown for 3 to 4 minutes. Drizzle them with honey and toss to coat everything evenly. Just when they begin to caramelize, deglaze with the orange, clementine, and lime juices. Bring to a simmer, then add the chicken stock, the remaining thyme,

and the cooking juices that have drained from the duck while resting. Cook 5 to 6 more minutes before adding the cider vinegar. Simmer gently for 5 to 8 minutes.

8. Strain the sauce through a sieve into a small saucepan, pressing down on the vegetables and trimmings to release their juices. Bring the sauce to a boil and taste for seasoning. Add the reserved citrus zest. If needed, add another tablespoon of cider vinegar for a nice lift. Simmer until the sauce coats the back of a spoon, then whisk in the butter, a few nuggets at a time. Remove from heat and keep in a warm place until ready to use.

9. To serve, carve the duck by removing the legs first and then the breasts. Arrange the meat on a warm platter, drizzle half the sauce over the duck, and pour the rest in a gravy boat. Serve immediately.

Chapter 9

FRANCE HAD GIVEN me a lasting parting gift: to leave a place with longing in your heart to return. Knowing I would always come back to the place where I had learned my craft, I flew home to America, anxious to begin work in a kitchen where I could learn more. Showing up to interviews with my knives in a canvas pouch, I went from one restaurant to the next. One chef used the interview as an opportunity to catch up on his *mise en place,* piling shellfish in front of me to shuck, then asking me to fill in for a prep cook who had called in sick. I quickly learned that this is the norm for kitchen interviews: Nine out of ten times, all you have to do is show up on time, ready to work, and you are hired. A résumé is superfluous— you can say you were the White House chef or an escaped convict and nobody will care. A nice suit or, *mon dieu,* nail polish? Forget about it. If you really want to work, show up in your uniform with your knives sharpened, keep your nails clean and trimmed, tie your hair back, leave your jewelry at home, and don't have plans for later. In most kitchens, there's a good chance they could use an extra pair of hands right away, and if they can't, you probably don't want to work there. Few working chefs have time to sit across a desk from you and ask about your hobbies (if you have any, don't mention them) and skills. Everything relevant becomes evident in the first fifteen minutes in the kitchen. If you have just one lazy bone in your body, it will sound a siren before you've tied your apron on. The chef who hired me was an apple-cheeked Englishman in a crisp chef's coat and a mile-high toque, who ran the kitchen of a landmark San Francisco hotel. He escorted me to his office, which was perched on stilts like a tree house, with glass windows overlooking a labyrinth of cooks. I desperately wanted to be a part of it. I was assigned a locker, then given a uniform and a time card.

Starting in the basement once again, I was assistant to Rosa, the garde-manger chef in charge of all the cold appetizers. A generous woman with a big laugh who easily shared her knowledge and skill, she called me *hija,* daughter, but her tone was no-nonsense. I thrived under Rosa's watchful eyes. She taught me everything without the assumption that I already knew certain things. The reality was that I didn't know anything. Those recipe index cards from my Cordon Bleu studies were of no use to me in a real kitchen.

Little by little, I learned to work in Rosa's station, where I quietly assembled what at first seemed astonishing quantities of hors d'oeuvres: fifteen hundred cherry tomatoes stuffed with mozzarella, three thousand salmon blini, cheese boards like ocean liners, cascading with clusters of grapes and wheels of cheese the size of car tires. I learned to carve tropical fruit towers with pineapple turrets, apple swans, tomato roses, melon boats. On Rosa's day off, I would follow her list but leave out the birds and the boats, presenting the pâtés, the charcuterie, the cheeses, simply, on slabs of marble or wood as I had seen in the markets in France. I wasn't trying to be smart; I had a different aesthetic and I didn't like to fondle a perfectly good apple to make it look like a bird.

When I was all caught up, I would be sent to Freddy, the pantry cook, who also happened to be Rosa's husband, but nobody was supposed to know or talk about it or the lady in human resources would make trouble. Freddy was a happy-go-lucky man who drove Rosa crazy for his lack of organization and inability to memorize the recipes he used every day.

Rosa, Rosa, please tell me how to make the Caesar dressing.
No! No way, Freddy! I showed you yesterday. You're stupid,
   Freddy, leave me alone.
Rosa, Rosa, ROSA! Please, mi amor, *tell me one more time.*
   Please, I'm a shit. I'm no good. Please, Rosa! I'm an ass-
   hole, good-for-nothing cabrón.
Goddamn you, Freddy! Asshole, asshole, asshole! I hope the
   chef fires your lazy ass. You can go live with your mama.
Rosita! I love you, Mama. You are my florecita.

But Freddy had a delicate touch composing his salads and sandwiches. He would often fall behind on the orders pouring in from room service, taking his time to warm the bacon for a BLT, or arranging hearts of romaine for a Caesar salad. The waiters hollered and banged their fists on the stainless steel shelf that divided them: Rápido, cabrón! *I'm coming around to kill you with my own two hands, you hear me?* Freddy would turn a deaf ear and whistle while he gingerly placed toothpicks in a club sandwich. I rushed around trying to help him catch up.

In Tehran, my mother would sometimes treat us to lunch at the Hilton Hotel coffee shop for Continental food. Each time, I would order a club sandwich and a vanilla milk shake, anticipating the miracle of that triple-decker triangle of bacon, poached chicken, mayonnaise, and tomato on toasted white bread, all held together with a frilly toothpick. My mother would smile approvingly at my choice, and inevitably someone at our table would express regret for not having ordered the same thing.

So Freddy taught me how to assemble my old favorite. I would confidently send him to lunch and offer to man his station. I thought I was being clever when I assembled a dozen clubs before the lunch rush, only to find the executive chef towering above me in his tall hat, his cheeks ablaze. He cleared his throat in a knowing way, before ordering me to take all those sandwiches I had proudly assembled to the staff cafeteria. *We assemble our sandwiches to order, mademoiselle.*

And I thought, *Ah, so that's why they behold that perfect combination of crisp and melt-in-your-mouth.* I was up to my neck in orders when I returned from delivering the clubs. I had so much to learn.

Rosa knew I would not stay long in her corner of the kitchen. When I was offered a promotion to line cook, I was afraid of what I didn't know, but Rosa shooed me over to the other side. It was not the hard work but the fire that made me doubt if I could take the heat. The first few weeks on the line, standing over twelve gas burners with the grill behind me, tested my mettle. The pace was alarming. It seemed as if everything happened at once and needed my attention then and there. I drank gallons of ice water and willed myself not to melt, while my colleagues, a team of middle-aged Chinese men, sipped green tea, checked a sauce, exchanged a joke, called an order, without so much as a bead of sweat on their brow. On my days off when I visited my parents, my mother gaped at the ladder of burns on my arms and swallowed her gasps. My father simply refused to look. *What sort of idiot would do that for eight dollars an hour?* We ate in silence, and after dinner I fell asleep on their couch, the exhaustion pulling me down.

A year and a half went by before I felt ready to move on. I had overcome my fear of astronomical numbers: *One thousand crab canapés? No problem.* It was all a matter of organization, and I knew I could manage it. San Francisco's culinary scene offered an array of talented chefs, and I was anxious to work in one of their kitchens. I rented an apartment a block away from the Hyde Street cable car, which took me to my new job every morning. The city was all mine at six o'clock when I hopped on. The conductor made jokes and called me *sweetheart* as we made our slow descent downtown. It was an era of renaissance for hotel restaurants, where every hotelier sought a gifted chef to transform his coffee shop into a signature restaurant. I was fortunate to be working alongside such a chef at the Pierre at Le Méridien. Those months of folding croissant dough paid off. The chef saw Fauchon on my résumé and I was hired; he didn't have time to read what I had actually done there.

I thought I had come from a fast-paced, efficient kitchen, but within days it was clear that this chef had extraordinary standards for maintaining order and cleanliness. From the instant I picked up a clean coat and apron from housekeeping, I joined a marathon and never looked back. Before service began, it was a race to prepare our *mise en place,* and once the first order was called, we kept our heads down and reached in every direction at once. Mistakes were not forgiven, so we simply did not make them. It was enormously gratifying when a dish came together and sparkled for a moment before a waiter whisked it away. Imagine a pheasant wrapped in lettuce with truffles and braised in the rich, brown stock of its roasted bones. You used all your senses: you looked at it, touched it, and smelled it to know it was done, then lifted it out of its caramel pool, tasted the *jus,* adjusted it with a squeeze of lemon, and sliced through the lettuce wrap, its emerald leaves now translucent against a milky white breast, the scent of truffles begging you to come closer. You were made of stone if you didn't fall for this dish. I never tired of the pattern of assembling a dish, falling in love with it, sending it away. You shrug and start all over, but each time it feels different— you and your dish in perpetual courtship.

The intensity of working in a kitchen was addictive. I thrived on the fever and the pace. I survived on cookies and torn heels of baguettes. When I had a day off, life on the outside was jarring and I had trouble switching gears. I hadn't the slightest clue what new movies were out, what people were listening to or dancing to, what exhibits were at the museums. I managed only to watch reruns of *Taxi* or read every night before collapsing into uninterrupted sleep, unless I had nightmares. As if the daytime drama were not enough, kitchen nightmares would haunt me in my sleep, dreams where everything unraveled in an irreparable mess—tickets handed to me were written in a code I could not decipher, tidal waves rose inches away from where I stood facing the stove, empty walk-in refrigerators formed a treacherous maze. Increasingly I lost touch with friends, living an insular kitchen life, working longer hours, and advancing through the ranks of medieval kitchen hierarchies. Medical students experience this intensity, but few expect it to last past their residencies, unless they stay in the emergency room. In Iran, I had witnessed my parents live at this level of extreme fervor, vehement in their devotion to their patients. My father rarely remembered our birthdays or what grade we were in, often mixing up our names—not an unusual parental slip—but he never forgot a patient's name or diagnosis. He left early in the morning, smelling so fresh from his aftershave and taking hurried sips of tea, not to return until late in the evening, exhausted. After a long, hot shower, it was all he could do to keep his head from falling into his soup, never mind helping me with algebra. My mother's work in the hospital went hand in hand with raising her three daughters and managing her household. Later she juggled two or three jobs with various women's organizations at a zealous pace. Once I was on the school bus, she hit the ground like a spinning top, somehow doing the grocery shopping, making dinner, sewing a costume for a school play, and hemming my sisters' bell-bottoms, too. It wasn't ambition that drove them; they simply didn't know how else to work, and having watched them closely, neither did I.

Within a year, I was put in charge of Le Méridien's café, which served three meals a day plus room service. No longer an hourly employee, I worked eighty-hour weeks and I was ecstatic. I was given free reign to change the entire menu, going from standard Continental fare to crêpes and homemade granola for breakfast, grilled tuna *niçoise* salad for lunch, and homemade gnocchi with braised duck for dinner. It was a dramatic transition for a place where steak and eggs were served in the morning and *niçoise* salad meant an ice cream scoop of tuna salad with overcooked eggs and limp green beans. I had to train a staff rumored to be set in their ways, but enthusiasm is contagious and they could hardly complain when they saw me march in at 7:00 a.m., flip crêpes with them, prep for lunch, cook lunch with them, prep for dinner, cook dinner with them, and finally untie my apron at 10:00 p.m. We planted a garden behind the hotel and grew herbs and lettuces. We built a smoker out of an old plate warmer, packed it with apple wood, and smoked turkey breasts for club sandwiches—taking them to yet another level—and salmon for potato waffles with crème fraîche. I was having the time of my life, but I still had a nagging feeling that I was an amateur. I knew I had the right instincts, but my experience was narrow. I wondered if I could hold my own in a French kitchen, if I could write menus like poetry, revealing simple, known ingredients in a new light, instead of parading exotic combinations to fool and dazzle in an attempt to hide everything that I didn't know.

The Pierre often hosted chefs from France's one- or two-star Michelin restaurants. We would feature their menus and work alongside them. The likes of Michel Bras and Antoine Westermann, who these days have three-star Michelin restaurants in France, were teaching me how to make spaetzle, allowing me to brown their squabs, dice their tomatoes, fold their raviolis. It was a marvel to watch them bring together two or three ingredients in a dish that was stunningly sincere, as if celery root and marrow were meant to be partners underneath transparent sheets of ravioli. It made you want to smack the side of your head: *Of course!* Working beside them,

I couldn't help measuring my skill against theirs. I knew it wasn't magic they possessed, but magic they practiced.

For me, France was the only place I could hone my craft. When I consulted my mother, she reminded me that over the years I had not spent a penny of all my earnings other than paying rent. *Take your savings, pack your bags, go back to France, and work until your money runs out.* At twenty-seven, when my career was in full throttle, I deliberately brought it to a halt and decided to return to France, accepting a *stagiaire,* an apprentice position without pay, at a three-star Michelin restaurant.

The thought of his daughter's not becoming a doctor remained unbearable for my father, who refused to give up hope that I would come to my senses once this kitchen fever subsided. He remained obtuse about the necessity of a respectable profession. I could not have pulled off this *cookery scheme,* as he came to call it, if we had returned to Iran. We would have been the laughing stock of our community: *Ha, ha! Dr. Bijan sent his daughter to America to study medicine and she decided to become a cook instead!* He could not contain his outrage at my pending return to France to work without pay. *We have raised a fool!* I sensed that my mother, despite her continued support, was beginning to have her own reservations, too. Would I continue working dog hours with little pay and no weekends off? Would I ever get married and have children if I remained chained to a stove? If my scars made her cringe, how would a man bear to hold my hand? What sort of underground world was this? It was one they could never fathom and I would not let them see. Too gritty, too loud, sometimes vulgar, with enough characters for a vaudeville show—why add to their worries?

I felt I *must* prove to my parents that surely there was a chance of something emerging from my shocking breakaway from their expectations, something that I could be wonderful at. Would my father be open to seeing my dissent as a sign of an independent mind, even if he could never be happy about it? Or would he look at me and think, *I don't know you*?

Before my departure for France, my family became eligible for citizenship. We were due to be sworn in within weeks of one another and we each came to the ceremony with our own private thoughts about the significance of this final severing of ties with our homeland. Reading the Constitution, I was aware of a profound shift: the taking of an oath, and the turning away from another allegiance. But my ties to Iran were now purely emotional, a pledge to its memories, language, food, poetry, and landscape. After eight years, the other story, the story of uprooting and replanting, was ending, and an American tale was emerging. I joined a handful of fellow citizens in a classroom inside a government building, where we sat at school desks and recited the Pledge of Allegiance, making a promise I felt I had already made. There ought to have been more ceremony, but the afternoon was uneventful. I raised my right hand, and a half hour later I was racing back to work.

Soon after, I applied for my American passport. It was not unlike growing a set of wings. No longer would I be singled out at the airport or forced to wait in long lines for a visa; no longer would I be the subject of scrutiny. The agent who took my application asked me where I was going. When I explained that I was going to France to become a chef, his enthusiasm was genuine: *Wow, your parents must be so proud of you!* I was overcome with gratitude for his kind words, for my newfound freedom, my wings. For days I leafed through the pages of my precious passport, its significance becoming more profound as I considered the irony of leaving America on the heels of becoming a citizen. But of course, I would come back. This was home.

Potato Waffles with Crème Fraîche

. . . .

The first time I ate waffles was on a trip to Disneyland. Until then I had only been in love with the word waffle *and the warmth it implied. When my mother took me to the amusement park, we stayed at a Travelodge and ate breakfast at a nearby diner. Perched side by side on red vinyl stools, we ordered waffles. Two plates arrived with whipped cream and strawberries piled on top of the hot, golden cakes. We looked at each other and gasped. I just know she was thinking the same thing:* I can't wait to come back tomorrow! *The next morning, the waitress poured coffee in a brown mug and remembered how my mother liked it. This small gesture made us feel so welcome and somehow connected to this place—an unsung diner in the maze of Los Angeles—that for years we brought it up* (Remember the waffles . . .) *yet we hardly remembered the rides in the park.*

I made these savory waffles for brunch at the hotel's coffee shop, where we jump-started a tired menu in spite of dubious guests who didn't want us messing with their breakfast. They demanded that we dish out our sad stack of pancakes from the box mix that calls for only water, and garnish it with orange slices and curly parsley. There was an early morning showdown between the kitchen and the wait staff—they didn't want to face cranky businessmen who hadn't had their coffee yet. At the time, change meant everything to me; I lived for it and threatened to quit if they stood in my way. It's beautiful when you're young and have convictions, even if it's just about breakfast.

Serve these waffles warm, drizzled with crème fraîche, smoked salmon, chives, and a squeeze of lemon. And if Iranian caviar is available, what a New Year's Day treat.

Yields about 12 4-inch waffles

2 large Yukon Gold potatoes
3 large eggs
1½ cups buttermilk
4 ounces (1 stick) butter, melted
1½ cups flour
2 teaspoons baking powder
1 teaspoon baking soda
½ teaspoon salt
1 tablespoon sugar
¼ to ½ cup milk to thin the batter if needed

1. Peel and chop the potatoes into 1-inch cubes. Use a steamer to cook them over boiling, salted water until very tender, about 5 to 7 minutes. Steaming the potatoes prevents them from becoming waterlogged. Drain and transfer to a bowl to mash into a puree.

2. Whisk together the eggs, buttermilk, and melted butter.

3. Add the potato puree to the buttermilk mixture and mix well.

4. Combine the dry ingredients. Make a well in the center of
   the flour and add the buttermilk mixture, stirring just until
   smooth. If the batter is too thick, you can thin it with milk,
   adding ¼ cup at a time.

5. Let the batter rest at room temperature up to 30 minutes,
   or overnight in the refrigerator; the batter improves the longer
   it rests.

6. Pour about ½ cup of batter into a very hot waffle iron and
   bake until golden and crisp. Serve hot.

Crème Fraîche

1 cup heavy cream
2 tablespoons buttermilk

Warm the cream gently by bringing it to a low boil and removing from heat. Stir in the buttermilk and pour the mixture into a
clean glass bowl. Cover tightly and leave in a warm place, between
70°F and 80°F (I use my oven with the pilot light on), to culture
for 24 hours. Refrigerate the crème fraîche. It will continue to
thicken, though far more slowly.

Crème fraîche will keep refrigerated for about 10 days. If it
becomes too thick, you can thin it with more heavy cream.

Salmon Gravlax with Meyer Lemon and Tarragon

....

If you ask me, the best part of living in California is the Meyer lemon—a fragrant, smooth-skinned juice bomb, native to our back-yards. It's enough to make you cry when you see coarse, three-dollar lemons in stores elsewhere in the country. When our tree bears fruit, I pack these fragile lemons in Bubble Wrap and send them Priority to relatives on the East Coast. I'm counting on our lemonade stands to pay for college someday.

In late June, when wild salmon becomes available, gravlax is a nice alternative to smoked salmon. Curing it with salt and lemon peel lends a succulent flavor that pairs well with the potato waffles.

Serves 6

4 tablespoons kosher salt

2 teaspoons sugar

3 tablespoons fresh tarragon, chopped

3 Meyer lemons, zested

1 side (approximately 2 pounds) wild salmon fillet, skin on

½ cup extra-virgin olive oil

¼ cup Meyer lemon juice with pulp

2 medium shallots, sliced thinly

1. Two days before serving, toss the salt, sugar, tarragon, and lemon in a bowl. Lay the salmon on a long piece of foil. Rub the salt mixture on both sides of the fillet. Lay another piece of foil on top and neatly seal the edges. Place a weight on the fish, the equivalent of 5 to 6 pounds (6 cans on a tray will do; 2- or 3-pound hand weights work well, too) and refrigerate for 48 hours.

2. Rinse away the lemon and herb mixture under cold running water. Pat the fish dry with paper towels and lay on a platter. Brush generously with olive oil and pulpy lemon juice. Sprinkle with shallots. Cover and marinate overnight before serving.

3. To serve, slice horizontally into paper-thin slices and lay on a chilled plate, with fresh lemons, capers, and crème fraîche.

Chapter 10

WHEN I STARTED kindergarten, my mother dropped off a
hot lunch at the office in a three-tiered metal lunch box with
rice, stew, and fresh fruit. I attended the Lycée Razi, a French
elementary school where segregation manifested itself in
the order in which we were allowed to eat lunch. At noon,
the French children were escorted by our teacher to the cafeteria and promptly served a French meal. The Iranian children were lined up outside the cafeteria behind glass doors,
through which we witnessed our classmates enjoying their
lunch. Unaware of discrimination, we thought this was how
things were done, but our stomachs grumbled nevertheless.
We were allowed inside only after the French kids were done,
and were given the privilege of eating over their trash.

My mother was running late one afternoon. She came running with my lunch box directly to the cafeteria. She stood
frozen in place, her eyes searching for me among the crowd

of kids with faces plastered to the glass doors. I turned to see her raw rage. Grabbing my wrist, she marched us toward the principal's office, sputtering, *The nerve, the nerve of these people!* I burst out crying, frightened and certain that I had done something unspeakable, but she was too angry to reassure me. She left me on a chair outside the office, stormed inside, and slammed the door. I heard her yelling in French, spitting out words I didn't understand but later learned. *Who, monsieur, do you think you are? You are a guest in my country.* When she finally came out, her face was flushed. She smiled down at me and took my hand, gently this time, and walked us through the gate. Once beyond the gate, she knelt down to hold me and broke into a sob, rocking me against her and saying she was sorry over and over again. We went home, where she warmed my lunch and sat quietly across from me, folding and refolding the corner of a napkin. That evening, the principal called to reassure her that he had called a meeting to reassess the lunch-hour protocol, but my mother hadn't used up all her sharp words, warning him to tread carefully, as she was reporting him to the board of education. A week later I was enrolled at a different school. Later, through friends, we heard that the French and Iranian children were eating lunch together, albeit at separate tables.

With an American passport in my chest pocket, I arrived in the French village of Vonnas. My late-afternoon train pulled into the little station—just a set of tracks between fields of wheat—and I stepped onto the platform, pulling a suitcase that landed with a loud thud, breaking the stillness that greeted me. No one else got off, and no one was there to tell me to go left or right, so I went left, dragging my suitcase behind me. I had packed my knives, two pairs of pressed checkered pants, two starched chef's coats, two pairs of black Reeboks, T-shirts, socks and underwear, a parka, sheets, towels, toiletries, paperback books, a radio, notepaper and pens, and an alarm clock. At the first café I asked for directions.

My walking through a sleepy village with a noisy suitcase in tow made the local gendarme suspicious. He stopped me for identification: *Vos papiers, s'il vous plaît.* I thought he was joking. What was this, 1942? He held out his hand, his jaw set. I proudly pulled out my brand-new blue passport and the letter from Monsieur Blanc, the proprietor of the restaurant where I would be working. At the mention of Monsieur Blanc, his face softened: *Alors! Why didn't you speak up sooner, mademoiselle?* He threw my suitcase into the trunk of his car and gave me a ride to the *foyer des travailleurs,* the lodging house for migrant workers on the edge of town. A round and grumpy manager gave me the keys to my room on the fourth floor. Everyone was still at work when I made my way up the stairs. I had given up a good job and an apartment in San Francisco's Russian Hill, with a glimpse of the Golden Gate Bridge, for this plain and functional room with an army cot and a shared bathroom down the hall. It was a chance I had to take to set myself apart. There were no shortcuts to becoming the chef I wanted to be. I unpacked and made my bed with sheets from home, set my alarm clock on the stack of books, dusted the windowsill, and tuned the radio to hear some French banter. I stood on my bed to put my suitcase away on top of the closet, glad that it would stay there for a while. The house was essentially a dormitory, and though I never saw the other workers, the smell of the bathroom told me I was the only woman on that floor. I also knew there were no Frenchmen among the workers; the voices I heard through the thin walls, when they came home from work late at night, were the tired French of Arab immigrants. I had a sense of calm and well-being, perhaps from the knowledge that here, in these blocks of rooms, there were no degrees of separation. I was simply a member of the proletariat.

In the lingering daylight, I found my way to Restaurant Georges Blanc. The ladies at the front desk were unimpressed when I gave them my name and explained why I was there. Clearly I wasn't a client and therefore I merited an indifferent shrug before they told me to return the next morning at eight o'clock and ask for Chef Patrick. I stopped for a bite to eat at the village café before turning in early, resisting the urge to call home or ring Aunt Farah in Paris to solicit some tender words.

Introductions were quick the next morning. I was assigned to Marie, the only woman in a brigade of forty, who was in charge of the vegetables. In the farthest corner of the kitchen, she left me to shuck an enormous crate of fava beans next to some Japanese *stagiaires,* apprentices like me, who were shucking peas. They barely nodded at me but didn't waste time interrogating me in rapid-fire French: *Where are you from? What other three-stars have you done? What is your position in America?* They needed to know that I did not pose a threat to their status as pea shuckers. When I delivered the favas, Marie gave me a pan of steamed buttered frogs' legs to debone. At eleven thirty I followed the Japanese delegation to a back room where a long table was set for lunch. I took a seat among a flock of French boys, who elbowed me to help themselves to platters of something-from-nothing casseroles prepared for the staff meal. I waited my turn for the plate of leftover cheeses from the cheese cart and the thin caramelized apple tart that was to become a staple of my diet. At home I had never sat down to a staff meal, so this was luxurious, and mandatory. Nevertheless, we ate as though we were being chased by wild dogs—the boys quickly ducking out for a smoke before lunch service started.

I watched as everyone filed into the kitchen and took their positions around a massive island stove with Chef Patrick at the helm, arching his eyebrows and tugging on his apron like a chevalier. I hung back with the Japanese boys for the first few orders, but before long the familiar rush of tickets poured in. I flew to the plating area to take a place next to the young men and carefully helped assemble the components of a dish, perfectly cooked and passed down the line by each *chef de partie,* the person responsible for each station. Meat, gorgeously browned, would arrive from Mark. Fish was handed down from Bruno. Vegetables came glistening from Marie. Gilles hollered from the garde-manger when he had sent the cold appetizers. For the next two hours I kept my head down and dressed the plates, only looking over to the chef to make sure it was done correctly. When it was over, I resumed my position in the back and was told by astonished cooks that no rookie had ever walked on line without an invitation from the chef.

When we came back that afternoon after a short break, Marie was a little nicer to me, and we prepped more frogs' legs together. Until then she had been the only woman, so maybe she was glad for the company. She talked little, and I was grateful for that. We worked quietly, side by side, and when we were done she sent me to help with breaking down the ducks. I learned that every afternoon a nearby poultry farmer delivered Monsieur Blanc's ducks. They had been killed at dawn and lay intact in wooden crates. To take these birds apart, we first switched to ankle-length plastic butcher aprons, which weighed nearly as much as X-ray bibs. We walked around the stove with all the pilots on, holding the ducks up like dance partners and swaying them over the flames, the smell of their singed feathers clinging to us. It got a lot messier once we chopped the necks and took the legs and breasts off, scrubbing the blood that splattered on the white tiled corridor where we were lined up by the sinks. The breasts were cured for duck prosciutto, the legs were saved for confit, and the carcasses were roasted to make a dark stock. After the first day, I didn't ask anymore; I walked over to the crates and joined the waltz around the stove.

Once again at six o'clock the staff rushed to eat dinner. After the earlier warning of my unprecedented faux pas, I waited in the back and busied myself until suddenly I heard Chef Patrick call my name. I flew through the maze of cooks to take my spot. He cocked one eyebrow and I fell right into step with the assembly. Nobody said anything after that, and the boys from Japan wouldn't look at me.

In a letter to my parents that night I described the butchery in detail, even attempting a lame joke about its resemblance to surgery, which I later crossed out. Why torment my poor father? Instead I elaborated on the presentation of the duck prosciutto, sliced paper-thin and laid with ribbons of olive tapenade, a lattice of rose and inky black, like Persian tiles. Did my father miss the flavor of the classic winter stew *fesenjan,* made with wild duck, pomegranate, and crushed walnuts, which he favored in Iran? I asked. On occasion, knowing that *Doktor* loved this dish, his patients would bring him ducks from the countryside. He would bring them home and lay them lovingly on the kitchen counter. *Oh, for heaven's sake, not again!* cried my mother. Tired from a long day at work, she couldn't face breaking down the birds, juicing pomegranates, grinding walnuts, and the long, slow braising that followed. He gave her his dreamiest look, beseeching, offering to shell the walnuts, pluck the feathers, massage her sore feet. *I could butcher them for you in no time, Mommy,* I boasted in my letter, *and you could sit at the kitchen table with a cup of tea, giving me instructions.* It so happened that I did have the opportunity to learn this dish with her when I returned to America. We substituted supermarket chicken, which needed much doctoring to taste as rich and complex, but the pomegranates came from a neighbor's tree, and we had fun scooping out the seeds and eating them like popcorn sprinkled with salt and angelica.

Writing to my parents helped me document my days. Unlike a diary, it allowed a conversation that might have been strained had I attempted to tell these stories in person, testing my father's patience for ingenue observations—my mother would find them charming, but he would most likely mutter: *Oh, grow up, will you? The world is not a French pastoral landscape!* I told them about Chef Patrick's rage if he found a carton of cream with a teaspoon left in it, or even a bruised tomato in the trash can—his intolerance for waste, a valuable lesson I'd missed in cooking school. My letters were filled with anecdotes: the farmer who named all seven hundred of his goats Julie and arranged his miniature goat-cheese pyramids on straw mats for the restaurant's cheese cart; the two dozen crates of tomatoes we peeled, seeded, and slowly roasted overnight with sea salt and sugar; the mouthwatering assembly of the caramel apple napoleons; the famous *poulets de Bresse,* chickens from a nearby poultry farm, all named Bavarde (Chatty), which roamed the field just outside my window and later became fried chicken, the recipe handed down from Monsieur Blanc's mother, from the days when the restaurant was just a roadside inn serving la mère Blanc's home cooking. I stared long at the black-and-white photos of that era lining the restaurant corridors—a young Madame Blanc and her crew, all women, bent over a stove, stirring and skimming enormous pots with ladles, her son at her knee. I wished we had photos of my parents in the early days of the hospital, their earnestness captured—my mother in a fitted nurse's uniform, buttoned down the front and belted at the waist, her hair gathered under her cap, my father in a white doctor's coat, hands clasped behind his back, his stethoscope looped around his neck. But for a handful of pictures, our albums were left abandoned under the rubble of revolution.

It was at this time that I began to imagine the marriage of French and Persian flavors, conjuring wild menus in my head, like seared duck livers with sour cherries, or cardamom crème caramel with pistachio *tuiles*. Like a rumor, first whispered thirty years ago, those once-exotic flavors—pomegranate, saffron, cumin, cardamom—are as common as vanilla today. But at the time they were heralded by messengers like me, elbowing our way for space at the table. For me, it was an indication that I was acquiring French cuisine as a language to be mastered, understanding its structure and its nuances so I could play and dream fluently instead of always translating and losing the essence. So when Marie would say, *Pas mal,* I wouldn't think she meant *Not bad* and take it as a compliment, when in fact she meant, *It's just okay. It could be so much better.* I could sit with these young cooks and laugh with them at a joke, not just smile to be polite. The next step, cracking the joke, would be far more difficult.

Though initially the elite kitchen brigade was suspicious of the new American woman, they soon realized I was not a hobby chef and I wasn't doing research for an article. In my proper element, without the trappings of a title, I was free to work through the stations, learning the kitchen inside and out so that I could go wherever help was needed. We worked long hours, but it was remarkably freeing to work without distraction. We got one day off a week. There was nothing along the main street in Vonnas other than a café and a pharmacy, so I'd take my laundry on the train to Bourg-en-Bresse, the nearest town, stop for a crêpe, and catch the train home with my clean clothes. Back in my room, I would lay wrinkled chef's jackets under the mattress to press them—a trick my mother had taught me when we traveled. It was a focused, monastic life that suited me fine. In the kitchen, we communicated with movement and rhythm. There was no pressure to prove anything, just a shared instinct for what needed to be done. Once again, there was no preoccupation with belonging, because I already belonged here. In this remote French village, I could walk into town at dawn in my uniform with my knife pouch tucked under my arm, take my coffee at the café with all the other workers, and be greeted with the particular respect the patrons had for the "kids" who worked for Monsieur Blanc, the chef and proprietor of the restaurant that had put them on the Michelin map. Where else would the townsfolk wave, the gendarme beep his horn, and the pharmacist have special ointments for your burn? I felt linked to this village, and Iran might as well have been on another planet.

One day at lunchtime, Chef Patrick walked the phone over to me with a big grin on his face. I had a phone call, he said, from Antoine Westermann, the chef of Le Buerehiesel in Strasbourg. He was one of the visiting chefs I had worked with at the Pierre, and I had written to him asking if I might work for him after my apprenticeship at Georges Blanc. Everyone stopped eating, willing me to stay at the table to take the call. They listened intently as I made arrangements. I didn't realize it was such a big deal for a lowly *stagiaire* to receive a personal call from a prominent chef and be offered a temporary, un-salaried position. But that phone call elevated my status. Even the maître d'hôtel and the girls at the front desk, who until then had been aloof, gave me a nod every morning.

It so happened that a few weeks later Monsieur Blanc received a call from Michel Guérard, the chef of Les Prés d'Eugénie, a three-star restaurant in the Aquitaine region. He wondered if any *stagiaires* could be spared. Monsieur Blanc recommended me, knowing I had already circulated through his kitchen and was ready to move on. I was not expected in Strasbourg for another two months, and with this opportunity to work for Michel Guérard, in a region I knew would boast an entirely different range of ingredients, I fantasized about staying in France, traveling from kitchen to kitchen with my knife pouch in hand, my sleeves rolled up. I wasn't ready to give up the life of kitchen monk, and I wanted to suspend the future as long as possible. Going home meant command and commitment to *one* kitchen.

During my last week in Vonnas, I lingered over the tasks we all did together, standing around a great big butcher block: deveining lobes of foie gras, peeling and slicing apples for caramelized apple tarts, shaping whole wheat walnut *boules* for the bread baskets. During service I was an octopus, reaching to help in every direction. I wanted them to miss me. We had champagne on my last night. Even the boys from Japan raised their glasses, and Monsieur Blanc, who just the day before, in a rare moment of one-on-one, had taught me how to make his signature tomato vinaigrette, gave me a silver key chain of a chef's toque, which I still carry today. Though I felt they had already given me so much, to my knowledge, I was one of the few who received any token of appreciation from the house.

Eugénie-les-Bains was an even smaller dot on the map. I arrived on an afternoon in July when the Tour de France was passing through a nearby village, and there were noisy crowds on the main street, spilling out of the only café. I got a ride to the restaurant, where the staff rushed out to greet me, thinking I was a guest. They continued to be gracious when I told them who I was, and escorted me to the *vieux hôtel,* used for staff housing. I was offered room and board in an old farmhouse with high ceilings and bright green shutters. My room, simply furnished with an antique canopy bed, a washstand, an armoire, and a big square window overlooking the fields, was a palace compared to that in the lodging house in Vonnas. My mother would have loved this room. I did what I knew she would have done, first opening the shutters and leaning far out the window, putting my toothbrush in the porcelain cup by the sink, hanging my newly washed chef's jackets in the big oak armoire, leaving my book and radio on the nightstand. Whenever we traveled, she unpacked right away, as if it were forever. I changed quickly and went down to the kitchen, knowing they weren't expecting me until the following day. I knew the routine. I ignored the curious looks, grabbed a case of peas, and started shucking. Eventually it would be dinnertime, and I would introduce myself then.

Michel Guérard's food was radically different from Georges Blanc's, catering to the spa crowd from Paris. I had come from the land of butter and cream to that of herb-infused broths, olive oil, and steam. The ambience of his kitchen was more playful, with pickup soccer after lunch on the big lawn just outside the kitchen. The *sous-chefs* rode fancy motorcycles and played pranks. It took me a few weeks to relax and appreciate the lightheartedness of this brigade, but by then it was time to pack and head to Alsace, where I was to begin work at Le Buerehiesel.

In Strasbourg, my lodgings were in the garret of a small, family-run hotel across the river and down the road from the restaurant. I slept soundly under the sloped beams and watched the sun come up through a triangular window over-looking the backyard. For the first time in months, I had a little bathroom to myself, an incredible luxury. Every night when I came home from work, the proprietors washed and ironed my chef's jacket and hung it on the back of the chair where I sat every morning for breakfast: a steaming bowl of café au lait and a basket of baguette and croissants with plenty of butter and jam. To me it was the Four Seasons, and I never wanted to leave.

Monsieur Westermann was the kindest, most sincere man I had the privilege of working for. His kitchen was completely void of ego and showmanship. Enamored with Alsace, he saw himself as a mere vessel between the land and his table. I spent an entire morning riding around with him in his little Renault, searching for the best potatoes. We stopped at farms where farmers took us through their fields, raking dirt with their fingers to dig little muddy lumps for him to taste, all declaring: *Voici la meilleure pomme de terre du monde! Here is the best potato in the world!* And Monsieur Westermann would laugh and tell them how the guy down the road just claimed *his* were the world's best potatoes.

In this kitchen they weren't interested in giving me their prep work. I didn't have to shuck or peel anything. Every day I assisted a different *chef de partie,* each one meticulous, earnest, and eager to show me what he was working on, assembling luscious mackerel, potato, and crème fraîche terrines, or velvet raviolis, like pillows, filled with braised cabbage and frogs' legs. The pastry chef coaxed *kugelhupf* dough and soaked purple plums in port for his skillet tart. The salad chef carefully washed his tiny greens and herbs, drying them in old-fashioned wire baskets he spun around, his arms like windmills. Like their boss, these chefs were equally captivated by their *terroir.* During service I watched their rapture as they plated their parcels. From the corner of my eye, I caught Monsieur Westermann's tall frame bending to inspect every plate that left the kitchen, his shoulders twitching, his face contorted, eyes blinking wildly. His *sous-chef* was a burly Alsatian with a Stalin mustache, as jolly as they come, God help you if you screwed up—he spared no words, and hurled them in German. When we all ate together at the long picnic table outside the kitchen, he sat like our papa, making conversation with all sixteen of us, teasing the younger lads and mussing up their hair, asking after our families, scowling at a wrinkled uniform. Between the two of them, they ran a flawless kitchen you would never want to leave.

I finally understood the world these chefs inhabited. It wasn't until I had shared their roofs, their meals, their tasks, their worries, that it became obvious: they could never be anything but cooks. And that plain truth spoke to me. I had known it since I was five years old. I had known it as an awkward kid who found grace in the kitchen. In these men, I found kindred souls. They were revered for the work they did day after day, and it was the *only* work they could do. And because their work was linked to the land where they had grown up, their sense of place was true. You tasted it in their food: they still grated nutmeg into their spaetzle as their grandmothers had, and fried chicken as their mothers had taught them, and dug wild mushrooms from the forest where they had tagged along with their fathers. I faced a riddle: how would I remain true to my homeland when I had learned my craft like a Gypsy?

Letters to my mother, written dutifully during breaks between lunch and dinner service, expressed my desire to stay as long as possible. Recalling the chilling incident in my kindergarten schoolyard, I joked that I had broken the glass wall that separated me from the French kids. I was reluctant to leave this world, where we shared such fierce devotion to our métier, and I loved the sight of my starched white coat hanging on the back of a cane chair, waiting for me to get to work. But it was time to find *my* kitchen.

Purple Plum Skillet Tart

. . . .

I find that I tend to construct a meal backward. Where most cooks begin with a bird, or a fish, my square one will most likely be a fruit or a vegetable. I always browse the produce first, and something will wink at me—a gorgeous bulb of fennel, freckled apricots with a rosy blush, purple eggplants. The fennel may send me to Greece to make a stew à la grecque, with white wine, garlic, thyme, and saffron, to serve with grilled lamb chops. The eggplant will most likely send me to Iran, to make khoresht, *a rich stew with tomatoes, cumin, tart grapes, and preserved lemons that compliments beef, lamb, or chicken equally well. Serve it piping hot over steamed basmati rice and watch the faces around you soften.*

Stone fruits, such as apricots and plums, almost always send me to the Alsace region of France, where I have fond memories of the pastry chef at Le Buerehiesel making Alsatian tarts. These fruits have a short season, so it's inevitable that we'll enjoy them with every meal, saving the superripe ones for making jam and tarts. I love walking to the table with a skillet to present this dessert. Otherwise known as a clafoutis, *this rustic and uncomplicated fruit flan is traditionally made with cherries, but plums, apricots, pears, or raspberries are equally delicious. I prefer French prune plums for baking, as they don't get soggy and their flavor intensifies with cooking.*

Serves 6

1 cup blanched, toasted almonds
½ cup flour
A pinch of salt
6 large eggs, separated
1 cup sugar
1 cup sour cream
2 tablespoons butter
1½ pounds ripe prune plums, halved and pitted
2 tablespoons honey
1 tablespoon confectioners' sugar

1. Preheat the oven to 400°F.

2. In a food processor, grind the almonds finely with the flour and a pinch of salt.

3. In an electric mixer, beat the egg yolks with ½ cup of the sugar until pale and thick, about 4 minutes. Blend in the sour cream. Fold in the almond flour. Set aside.

4. Beat the egg whites with the remaining sugar until soft peaks form. Fold into the yolk mixture.

5. In a 10½-inch nonstick skillet over medium-high heat, melt 2 tablespoons of butter. Add the pitted plums and sauté for 2 to 3 minutes. Drizzle the honey to caramelize the plums, cooking for another 2 minutes. Drain any excess liquid. Pour

the almond batter over the plums and place the skillet in the center of the oven. Bake until the batter puffs up and turns a rich golden brown, about 15 to 20 minutes. If you prefer not to bake in the skillet, simply transfer the plums to a buttered ovenproof baking dish and continue with the previous steps.

6. Remove from the oven and preheat the broiler.

7. Sift confectioners' sugar over the tart. Place the skillet under the broiler about 2 inches from the flame. Broil about 1 minute, until the sugar is caramelized. You can also use a kitchen torch to caramelize the top.

8. Serve warm from the skillet with a dollop of soft whipped cream and a glass of chilled late-harvest gewürztraminer.

Tomato Confit

. . . .

*In Tehran, my mother made tomato paste in midsummer, when
she found crates of ripe tomatoes in the market. Jars of tomato paste
dried on the hospital roof until the first day of school. On long summer days, when I had nothing to do, I would sneak to the roof and
dip my finger into the jars to sample her paste. I couldn't resist making a dent in the red, velvety surface, and I held the pungent flavor,
at once salty, sour, and sweet, on my tongue as long as I could, like
tomato candy.*

*The next time I tasted anything similar was during my appren-
ticeship at Restaurant Georges Blanc, where every week we roasted
crates of tomatoes for* tomates confites. *Row upon row of wrinkled,
leathery tomatoes lined the kitchen, to appear later, layered in a
magnificent dish of buttered leeks and frogs' legs. I consider them my
best souvenir from that period.*

*When tomato season is in full swing, we gorge ourselves, and
near the end, making these tomato "candies" is a way to make them
last. With their infinite versatility, they are delicious on pizzas
with olives or anchovies, in scrambled eggs, with pasta, with grilled
fish or braised lamb, or with fresh mozzarella and eggplant in a
vegetarian lasagna—and sometimes simply drizzled with olive oil
and tucked into a crusty roll for a picnic on the roof.*

4 pounds (about 20) Early Girl or any medium-size
    vine-ripened tomatoes
1 cup extra-virgin olive oil
Kosher salt
3 tablespoons sugar
6 cloves garlic, crushed
8 sprigs thyme

1. Preheat the oven to 250°F.

2. Core and peel the tomatoes, then halve them horizontally.
   Gently squeeze the halves or use a small spoon to remove the
   seeds. Strain the seeds and pulp to recuperate the tomato juice
   to use for sauce or soup.

3. Prepare 2 baking sheets by lining them with parchment paper
   and brushing with some olive oil. Sprinkle 1 tablespoon of salt,
   2 teaspoons of sugar, and the garlic on each sheet pan. Place
   the halved tomatoes, cut side down, on the seasoned pans,
   close together but not stacked. Brush the tops with more olive
   oil and season with salt and 2 more teaspoons of sugar. Tuck
   the sprigs of thyme in between the rows.

4. Place the tomatoes on the middle racks of the oven and roast
   for 4 to 6 hours. They must cook slowly at a low temperature
   to dry and candy. Check to see if they have released a lot of
   juice about halfway through, and if so, remove the pans from
   the oven and use paper towels to soak up the extra liquid.

Return the pans to the oven and continue cooking. Turn your oven down if the tomatoes have browned but remain watery.

5. Remove the tomatoes from the oven when they have a leathery texture and are deep red. Once cooled, they are ready to be used or stored. Use clean glass jars or porcelain dishes to store them, drizzling the remaining olive oil on the topmost layer and sealing tightly. They will keep up to 2 weeks refrigerated, as long as a clean utensil is used to take what is needed with each use.

Note: You may also prepare the tomatoes as shown in steps 2–3 and roast overnight at a lower temperature, in a 200°F oven.

Chapter 11

LEARNING TO COOK is like learning to speak a language with ease and confidence so that you can tell a joke without tripping, sing a song without missing a beat, dream in that language, and wake up with a menu dancing in your head as you run to collect eggs, butter, flour, sugar, and salt to make dough you shape into the moon and stars for a child's birthday party.

Paris, San Francisco, Tehran, all claim a part of me. As I looked out the window on the plane home from Paris, I thought about how the kitchens where I was shaped belong to all these places, and yet none claim to be the center. I'll always negotiate that in-between culture. And I'll always rely on the longing for these places, and I'll always be learning to move between them without falling through the gaps.

When my mother picked me up at the airport, I asked her if she wouldn't mind taking me to San Francisco so I could look at the Sherman House, a beautiful hotel that sat like a wedding cake on an ordinary street in the posh neighborhood of Pacific Heights. *Now?* she asked. *Yes, now, just a quick peek.* I had walked by it numerous times and had entertained unlikely thoughts of maybe someday being the chef there. I knew the Swiss chef who ruled the kitchen; I had actually worked under his thumb for a fortnight but had politely resigned because I couldn't follow his formulaic approach, which left no room for imagination. Years later I wrote to the proprietors from France, expressing my interest in returning, but this time as the executive chef. I felt as if everything I had ever done was meant to prepare me for this job, in this kitchen. My mother knew they had offered me a position and she was familiar with its exclusive reputation. She understood my need to take another good, long look at the place from the outside. It was late afternoon when she parked across the street, and we watched the white turn to pink in the waning light. One by one, the lights came on in the rooms, a taxi dropped off a lady with shopping bags, and a butler ran to help her in. I felt my mother's eyes on me. *I won't see you much once you start working here, will I?* We sat there till after dusk before driving home, but I could hardly wait to go back.

The proprietors took a risk and turned their kitchen over to me, even though they were already well known for the classic cuisine of their former chef. Their firm faith in me was an essential component to our success. There was no other way to reinvent this kitchen but to be bold and to work long, hard hours. My apartment was a fifteen-minute walk away, and I would often break into a run for the last few blocks, frustrated that my legs couldn't get me there faster, always stopping for just a minute to gaze up at the hotel, still incredulous that its kitchen was mine.

I was in the basement again and I loved every inch of that four-hundred-square-foot kitchen, with its flight of stairs that took you up to the gardens. Backed by a charged, muscular crew, I cooked the way my father practiced medicine—with joy, precision, heart, and soul. My *sous-chef,* a gifted pastry chef, was equally uncompromising. We fell in step from day one and cross-trained our staff, not allowing anyone to become too specialized. Dishwashers learned how to make everything from croissant dough to truffles. Like humming-birds, we flew between stations. We all washed dishes, we all took the stove apart and scrubbed it. We never quit, and no one dared to call in sick unless they were in the hospital.

Just weeks after I started, the Loma Prieta earthquake shook the soup bowls off the shelf. At five o'clock, I was making jam thumbprint cookies, expecting a party of fifty at six. Potatoes roasted in the oven, mushrooms simmered in red wine, and Ricardo, one of our prep cooks, was dipping candied orange peel in chocolate. I heard what sounded like the telephone, but it was the shrill of silver bowls rattling as they slid off the shelf. I yelled for someone to answer the phone—we had a three-ring rule—but everyone rushed past me out the door. The boy delivering our bread dropped the bag of rolls and dashed back out, and I looked down to see dinner rolls bouncing like Mexican beans. I still hadn't figured out what was happening and I was annoyed with the bread man. I looked through the back door to find everyone, including the general manager, standing bewildered on the street.

The Bay Bridge has collapsed! Until I heard that, I wasn't convinced that our party wouldn't show up. As we rushed to turn the gas off and calm our hotel guests, I thought about my cousin, Kimya, who had just recently moved to San Francisco and was staying with me until she found her own place. It was October and already dark; I hoped she would find the candles in the kitchen drawer. I thought of my parents, unable to reach me, and how worried they must be. Literally shaken out of their rooms, the guests gathered in the lobby. We opened the bar and made platters of food, as did most of the restaurants in the city that night. A few hours later, they told me my cousin was at the front desk. Somehow, in the dark chaos, she had found her way to me, her eyes wide as saucers. I made her a plate of cheese and crackers while I struggled to ice down everything in the walk-in refrigerator. Eventually we walked home, holding hands in the pitch black. On the busy intersection of Van Ness and Green, a man in a ball cap was directing traffic. Everyone was outside on the street with bottles of wine and stories: *Where were you when it happened? I was at the Laundromat. I was walking my dog. I was washing dishes.* We stopped to listen and offer our own account: *I just moved here from Kansas City!* By the time we reached my apartment, we weren't surprised to see my neighbors—the human faces of my building, until now anonymous—perched on our front stoop, offering us a beer. That night, I learned their names.

Over the next few days it seemed as if we were always searching for coffee. A café in the neighborhood had a generator, and we joined a line that looped around the block to take coffee to the hotel guests who were rushing to check out. Once we had power, Kimya sat in a trance, watching TV coverage of the damages. She made anxious calls home, and my mother urged us to come stay with them. Neither of us slept through the night, but we never considered leaving the city. It was a period I would look back on with wonder, because for the first time in years I was forced to slow down. It took an earthquake for me to eat dinner with my cousin, the same one who had consented to relentless hours of playing Barbie when she was seven and I was nine, the same one I had coerced into memorizing lines for our plays, the same one who painstakingly glued together the plates and bowls that had slid off my shelves. As annoyed as I was for the disruption the earthquake had caused, it had offered a respite. Once we resumed our routines, she found an apartment, and I returned to the insular world of my kitchen.

Finally given the freedom to develop my own style, I was able to draw from my Persian, French, and American pantry, coaxing partnerships and matchmaking, not for the sake of novelty, but because I couldn't help being a sum of those cuisines. I refused to have specialties. I disdained the notion of cooking as art, or any reference to it as "my food." And I couldn't imagine a private life, one separate from my kitchen. I didn't have a boyfriend. I didn't shop. I didn't go to parties. Happiest standing by my stove, I appreciated the recognition that came in due time, but I didn't have the temperament for stardom, afraid it would take me away from my kitchen.

At twenty-eight, I was oblivious to pop culture. When Bono and his family checked in one afternoon, one of the waiters bolted down to the kitchen to let me know. He was trembling in his tuxedo, beads of sweat gathered on his forehead. James played bass in a band; seeing Bono was like seeing Jesus walk through the front door of the hotel and ask for a room. He mistook my blank expression for shock, stammering:

> I-I-I know. *Can you believe it? I-I-I'm speechless. Help me.*
>   *Oh God!*
> *You mean Sonny Bono? Who cares? Pull yourself together,*
>   *man.*

This was too much for him. He raced out to find someone to commiserate with, someone from 1990, not 1977. Later that afternoon, Bono's wife stopped by the kitchen to ask if I could warm her baby's bottle. Quiet and sweet, she stood by and waited while the bottle bobbed in a pot of simmering water. In the evening, James held their dinner order in a sweaty palm. While I cooked their dinner, he prepared their room-service tray, lovingly polishing the silver domes and cutlery that rattled in his hands. *What a racket,* I thought. *How's he going to carry that upstairs?*

You're going to have to make two trips, James. Shall I come with you? He assured me he had everything under control. That look of rapture never left his face. I had no one to blame but myself when I heard the deafening crash a few minutes later. Down went the rack of lamb, the scallop and blood orange salad, the lemon tart, the bowl of raspberries. It was like a Marx Brothers movie, only humorless. The next morning, I called a friend: *Who is this Bono?* I asked, still pronouncing it like "no-no." *Ever heard of him?*

At home, my mother was doing her share of matchmaking, introducing new ingredients into her Persian dishes, adjusting temperaments and intensities, substituting cranberries for barberries in a classic saffron rice dish with slivered almonds and pistachios, roasting Halloween pumpkins for a veal shank stew. I tried to call her every day for a quick hello, and our conversations inevitably fell to the topics of food and men. Apparently, ancient aunts were calling her with names of suitable mates for me, interested parties, new crops of graduates, like freshly harvested fruit for Donia *joon*'s inspection:

Darling, your auntie Haleh called.
Oh?
Yes. She said Dr. so-and-so's son is graduating from Stanford
    Medical School.
Good for him!

Do you remember him?

You mean that short kid with the really high voice?

Not so short anymore. And *he's looking for a wife.*

Wish him good luck for me, Mamani. *I have to go now.*

Baby, remember Dr. so-and-so's son, Shahin?

The hairy one?

He's going to law school at Berkeley.

So?

Auntie Jamileh said he read about you in the paper.

So?

Do you want to meet him for coffee sometime?

What for?

What for, what for. To exchange recipes!

Seriously, how boring.

What makes you *so interesting?*

Nothing.

Then you'll have so much in common!

So, did you ever try the pomegranate molasses?

Don't change the subject!

Apparently the French boys' assessment of me was proving true: no baker, no doctor, no lawyer was going to derail the old girl. I had only just begun. After four years at the helm of the Sherman House kitchen, I had received hearty accolades, and the desire to open a restaurant of my own increased. I couldn't shake the idea of a sweet little French bistro—its wood-paneled interior, its chalkboard menu, its zinc bar, its starched white napkins, its sound spilling out onto the side-walk every time someone opened the door—like the ones I used to gaze at so longingly on the streets of Paris.

In the last few weeks of my tenure, the hotel proprietors invited my parents to dinner. My father's health had been deteriorating—stress, fatigue, and disappointment had given way to disease. He had survived heart attacks and heart sur-geries, but the final diagnosis of Parkinson's sentenced him to the weary walls of his ravaged body. My mother had recently retired and was taking care of him full-time. Once again, faced with despair, she showed her absolute resolve.

I was so proud that my parents would finally eat in the dining room where I had lovingly cooked thousands of meals for others, but never for them. I had lived and worked like a monk, deliberately leaving them out of my world in a fever-ish race to be really good at something, and when my mother finally pulled up to the curb where I stood waiting for them in the rain, I wept. When they saw me crying, they started to cry, too. The owner, rushing to greet them, stood by and let the three of us cry on the sidewalk in the rain.

I wrote a menu that read like a love letter, with quotes and poems tucked within its lines, its pattern evocative of a Persian carpet, following a different sequence of flavors but telling a familiar story, like the carpets we had left behind depicting water, trees, birds, harvest, home, hope. This was a chance to show them the patchwork quilt I had made with the threads they had given me. I made sweetbread schnitzels with lemon and capers, braised endive with honey, wrapped duck with dates in tender cabbage leaves, quince sorbet, and rose petal ice cream, mindful of the portions so my father wouldn't need a knife. My hands trembled like my father's—they always did when I cooked for loved ones—and I didn't want him trying to cradle a knife in his quivering fist. There were eleven courses. My mother sent a note with her plate after the sixth course was cleared: *Bravo, my girl!* Just like the notes she used to tuck in my lunch box and my apron pocket.

Roast Duck Legs with
Dates and Warm Lentil Salad

* *

This is a favorite fall dish, when pomegranates hang heavy like impossible red bulbs from skinny branches. As kids, we used to squeeze their leathery skin to crush the seeds to a pulp, then poke a hole with a fork, run outside to avoid dripping on the carpet, and tip our heads back to suck the juice. It was the ultimate juice box.

I use dates for this dish—an homage to an old French dish, canard aux pruneaux, duck braised with prunes—for the generous flavor of molasses they lend to the sauce. I love to serve it with a lemony watercress salad tossed with just a few roasted, crushed pistachios to break the richness of the sauce and wake up your palate.

Serves 6

6 Muscovy duck legs
Kosher salt and fresh-ground pepper
1 medium yellow onion, diced
1 carrot, diced
1 stalk celery, diced
2 whole cloves
1 bay leaf
1 tablespoon honey or pomegranate molasses if available
3 sprigs thyme
1½ cups pomegranate juice
2 cups duck or any poultry stock

4 tablespoons olive oil

2 cups green French lentils

1½ cups Medjool dates, pitted

1 tablespoon red wine vinegar or pomegranate vinegar

1. Trim the fat from the edges of the duck legs. Rinse and pat them dry. Season both sides with salt and pepper and refrigerate overnight.

2. Preheat the oven to 325°F.

3. Pat dry any excess moisture from the duck legs. In a large skillet over medium heat without oil, brown the duck legs, skin side down, until golden, about 8 to 10 minutes. As the duck browns, it will render fat. Turn the legs over and cook 3 or 4 minutes on the flesh side. Remove from the skillet and arrange them snugly, skin side up, in a roasting pan.

4. Pour off the excess fat, keeping just 1 tablespoon in the skillet to sauté half the diced onions, carrots, and celery. Add 1 clove, the bay leaf, 1 tablespoon of honey, and 2 sprigs of thyme. When the vegetables are translucent, add the pomegranate juice and simmer 10 minutes. Add the stock and reduce for 10 minutes. Pour around the duck legs to a depth of about 1 inch. Cover well and place in the center of the oven for 1 hour.

5. While the duck is braising, cook the lentils: Sauté the remaining onions, carrots, and celery in 2 tablespoons of olive oil

over medium heat. As the vegetables soften and begin to turn golden, add the clove, salt, a sprig of thyme, the lentils, and about 3 cups of water or duck stock if you have extra. Bring to a gentle boil and reduce the heat to a simmer, cooking the lentils uncovered and adding water (or stock) just as the lentils absorb the liquid. Cook about ½ hour (if using brown lentils, they may cook more rapidly), until they are tender and coated with their liquid but not swimming in it. Taste for salt. Keep at room temperature.

6. Remove the duck legs from the oven and turn them over. Tuck in the dates. Cover the roasting pan and return to the oven.

7. After 30 minutes, turn the duck legs back over, skin side up, and increase the oven temperature to 400°F. Let cook, uncovered to brown the legs, for about 20 to 25 minutes.

8. Remove the pan from the oven and let rest a few minutes. Gently arrange the duck legs and dates on a platter. Skim the fat from the cooking liquid and pour into a saucepan. If you're short on sauce, add a little stock. Set the pan over medium heat, bring to a gentle boil, removing any foam that rises to the surface, and lower the heat to reduce the sauce until it coats the back of a spoon.

9. Warm the lentils and stir in 2 tablespoons of olive oil and the red wine or pomegranate vinegar. To serve, spoon the lentils onto a platter as a bed for the duck legs with the dates perched in between. Dress each leg with 1 to 2 tablespoons of sauce.

Rose Petal Ice Cream
. . . .

This ice cream, reminiscent of a scent more than a flavor, is what I imagine people who have fallen in love ought to eat. It is new and fresh, evocative and mysterious. It is not vanilla.

Makes 2 quarts

2 cups fresh garden rose petals
8 egg yolks
1 cup granulated sugar
2 cups heavy cream
2 cups milk
1 tablespoon rose water

1. Wash the rose petals and pat them dry between 2 towels.

2. In a large stainless steel saucepan, immerse the petals in the milk and cream. Scald, then turn off the heat to let the petals steep in the hot milk. Strain the milk after 20 minutes. Discard the petals and return the milk to the saucepan. Over low heat, bring the milk just to a boil and turn off.

3. Whisk the egg yolks with the sugar until the sugar dissolves and the mixture turns pale yellow. Pour about ¼ of the hot milk into the yolk mixture and whisk continuously while slowly adding the remaining milk. Return to the saucepan and cook over low heat, stirring continuously with a wooden spoon until it thickens and coats the back of a spoon.

4. Strain through a fine mesh strainer into a bowl. Whisk 2 or 3 times to release the heat. Stir in the rose water. Chill the ice cream base in the refrigerator for 2 to 3 hours.

5. Freeze the mixture in an ice cream machine, according to the manufacturer's instructions.

6. Serve in chilled glasses garnished with fresh rose petals, or scoop into a sugar cone and share with the one you love.

Chapter 12

LIKE EVERY CHEF, I held on to the dream of having my own place. Everything I had done was meant to prepare and train myself for achieving this goal. So clear was my vision of what this place would be, that I could hear the sounds, the chatter, the calling of tickets. I could feel the warm bodies huddled around steaming bowls of coq au vin, mopping up the juices with torn bread, raising their glasses of red wine. I twitched with the longing to feed them, to gather them under my roof. I wanted to own, not just the china and silver, but also the scars, the praise, their appetites.

When a neighbor found my father wandering one afternoon, she brought him home just as my mother had spiraled into panic, screaming his name throughout the neighborhood in her search to find him. Coming to terms with the astonishing rate of his memory loss, she swiftly decided to move to a gated complex. The funds from the sale of their home, plus vast contributions from my sister's paychecks, went toward the lease and renovation of an eighteen-hundred-square-foot space that became my restaurant, L'Amie Donia. If ever you find yourself with the extraordinary good fortune of coveting a lifelong dream aligned with the fervent support of your family, know that it is an unparalleled gift.

The intensity of kitchens past was a honeymoon compared to opening and operating a restaurant of your own. Every day tests your resolve and stamina. Every day you are thrown a dozen curveballs, which you'd better catch because there is no mercy if you happen to look the other way. My sister left her own kids at home to watch my back like a mama bear, keeping a vigilant eye on the front of the house, placating disgruntled guests who had waited too long for tables, buffering the tension that built up once the doors opened. Her firm hold allowed me to march forward with a battery of *sous-chefs,* one in particular who blasted Annie Lennox, the Pretenders, Sinéad O'Connor, and Madonna from speakers perched on the beams, sound tracks to propel our forward motion. Others sustained the motion with humor, wit, and creamy bowls of polenta. Our maître d'hôtel had spent her youth in France and knew instinctively how to keep my vision intact without compromise, orchestrating the dining room with impeccable savoir faire. And underneath this beautiful collaboration, we still shuddered with anxiety when the doors opened every night. Vitamins, coffee, service. Vitamins, coffee, service. Push-ups, coffee, service. A grease burn. Cold beer buried under ice—drink it or pour it on your wound. Clean up. Call orders for the next day. Go home. Get a Band-Aid. Collapse. Get up. Do it again. Do it again. Do it again.

I wondered if the fright and exhilaration was similar to what my father had felt when he opened the doors to his hospital. Were people waiting on the sidewalk, anxious with pregnant wives, kidney stones, and broken bones? Was he ready? Did he have enough beds? Had he been impatient, like me, with the inspections and permits, contractors and electricians, to hurry up so he could let people in? By the time I opened my restaurant, it was too late to ask him. He didn't know me. There was strange comfort in the realization that he no longer knew who I was: I was his sister, the pharmacist's wife, the hospital cook. I was the nurse from his clinic. I was no one.

It was a rare occasion when my mother asked for help, but one time when she had a doctor's appointment, she asked if I could watch my father for an hour. I was a coward, afraid of being left alone with him. I harbored years of reproach and couldn't face an old man who had long ago stopped shouting and calling us names. I found him sitting rigid on the couch with a blanket over his knees, stacking beads, the shaking in the right fist hammering them away. I sat next to him and kissed his soft jowl, smelled his Nivea cream—his absence of expression an antidote to my hot tears. I couldn't ask him about his hospital, its terraced rooms, its rambling gardens. I couldn't ask him about his patients, waiting for their hero to make his rounds. I could not remind him of his Caspian Sea, the salt air, or the song he sang to us in the car. The tide had pulled away all the sounds, including the words I'd never said to him. This surgeon who had cut into bodies with sharp knives and peered in, sewn them back up, and sent them on their way, had retreated quietly to a wide-open field where he had cleared his mind and folded away his expectations, along with his disappointments, his knowledge, and his memories.

My mother tended to my father lovingly. She washed and dressed him and frequently wheeled him to a patio table reserved for Maman and Papa Bijan, where she spoon-fed him potato leek soup, wiped his chin, and murmured my praises. She kept a scrapbook of every article, photo, and mention of me in the paper and read it softly to him, gripping his hand as if he might get away. Tethered to her voice and her touch, and the warmth of the soup, he responded with a flutter of his eyelashes, the blue in his eyes no longer stormy, just bright.

When we had time for a chat, my mother critiqued my menus and reminded me of dishes we had made together in Tehran, Paris, Majorca. These conversations inevitably found their way into the next day's menu—a paella with saffron rice and Gulf shrimp, a fig tart with cardamom ice cream, roasted stuffed quince with homemade fennel sausage. And this food brought the people. My restaurant thrived under the overwhelming enthusiasm and appetite of our customers, who waited patiently by the entrance when we didn't have enough chairs.

My father did not have the funeral he would have had in Iran—shopkeepers closing up to attend his service, silver platters of halvah and saffron pudding offered to mourners, car after car following his coffin. He would have liked that. His long illness had left my mother bereft and aching. She feared she had not loved him enough, cared for him well. She sorted his clothes and set aside special items for his sons-in-law—a soft suede jacket, an alligator belt, treasures that were exclusive to him, saving a watch and his favorite Russian sheepskin hat for her soon-to-be son-in-law. I was engaged after a long courtship to a young American painter, a man attentive to details in the world, uncompromising and devoted to his work, without a trace of cynicism, and brave despite all the odds against him. When I met him, he was subsisting on whole milk and cookies, living in a piano crate a clever landlady had transformed into a "cottage" for rent on her property, and saving every penny to go back to Europe to paint. *Oh, a dreamer like me,* I thought, *acting like the world is his for the taking.* He proposed to me on a sidewalk in Paris, where we had met over the Christmas holidays when the restaurant was closed. While warming my hands in his with quick, warm breaths, he placed his mother's ring in my palm. Leaning into each other was home. It did not escape us that my father would have hollered and made threats had he remembered what a painter was. A cook was bad enough.

My mother could not be idle. Although we tried to keep her busy and fulfill some of her lifelong wishes, one being to see an opera at the Met, *Tosca* didn't offer meaningful work. After years of nursing her children, her patients, her husband, her purposeful life had come to a halt and there was no one to look after. Not one for rest, she wouldn't allow herself a cup of tea until she had scrubbed the kitchen and swum her laps, nor could she watch the news passively and go back to her knitting. It wasn't long before she volunteered for an international medical corps that sent her to Kosovo during the war. Her selflessness proved too much for some, who criticized her altruism: *Who does she think she is, Mother Teresa?* I imagine her fortitude embarrassed them: *What is she trying to prove?* It made my blood boil to hear these people forsaking her for showing them what they despised in themselves. Her motives were far from sanctimonious; if anything, she was impulsive, like a child who stops to point at a homeless man and ask, *Why? Why is that man sleeping under the eaves of the library?* She couldn't walk by a wilted potted plant, much less pretend that the horror on the front pages had nothing to do with her. She downplayed her efforts in the Balkans, fibbing that she was comfortably housed in modern apartments in Priština, when in fact, at seventy-two, she was staying in a tent and delivering a new generation of Kosovars in refugee camps. All of us had come to *expect* heroism from her.

News of a grandchild on the way stirred a flurry of activity: sweaters and caps to be knit, layettes to be sewn. She hurried home from an assignment in Moldova, where she was training nurses, bringing with her a selection of hand-painted wooden toys. I then became not her daughter but the mother of her grandson, and one she had to nourish and command. Driving with her, I was not allowed to exceed ten miles an hour. And when I called her early one morning, she knew before I had spoken a word: *You're in labor. I'll be there in five minutes!* Did she intend to deliver my baby? I wondered. In fact, hours later in the delivery room, she called my doctor and scolded him for being late: *Do I have to deliver my own grandson, Doctor?*

There is a photograph of my mother holding her American grandson next to the *haftsin,* the traditional table set for the Persian new year, celebrating the vernal equinox—his due date. Arriving early, a week before Noruz, he granted us the best new year's gift. Her tablecloth displays seven dishes that herald spring and rebirth: *sib,* an apple symbolic of health; *sabzeh,* wheat or lentil sprouts, which represent the rebirth of nature; *seer,* garlic, a tribute to health; *sekeh,* coins for prosperity; *senjed,* the dry fruit of a lotus tree, symbolic of love; ground sumac, which mirrors the color of sunrise; and *serkeh,* vinegar, representing the wisdom of age. There are other components to the *haftsin,* such as a flowering hyacinth, a candle lit for every child in the family, a bowl of painted eggs, a goldfish, a volume of poems by Hafez, and a mirror to reflect everything we hope for in the new year, to be mindful and present. Swaddled, my son sleeps in her arms, and in her wet eyes, I read, *Here you are, here you are, at last.*

Roasted Stuffed Quince
with Fennel Sausage and Currants

. . . .

*When I make this dish, I feel as if I am reaching far back in time.
It is one of the oldest recipes—this unique combination of rich
meat and tangy fruit, which dates to pre-Islamic Persia, when the
principles of Zoroastrian harmony applied to every aspect of life,
including food. There are dozens of Persian recipes that achieve
this delicate balance of opposing flavors and textures, like a good
marriage—surprising and complementing one another. My addition of fennel seeds, currants, and cider is a nod to the past and
the present.*

Serves 6

1 cup dried currants

1½ cups apple cider

¾ cup split peas

6 medium quinces

1 medium yellow onion, diced

1 celery stalk, diced

1 carrot, diced

6 tablespoons unsalted butter

½ pound ground lamb

1 teaspoon fresh thyme leaves

1 teaspoon fennel seeds

1 teaspoon cinnamon

2 cups beef or chicken stock

1 tablespoon bread crumbs

1 tablespoon honey

1 tablespoon cider vinegar

A pinch of saffron

1 whole allspice

6 whole cloves

Kosher salt and fresh-ground pepper

1. Soak the currants in apple cider for 30 minutes. Strain the currants and reserve the cider.

2. Cook the split peas in 2 cups of water and 1 teaspoon of salt for 40 minutes, until tender. Drain and set aside.

3. Wash the quinces and cut a ¼-inch "hat" horizontally from the top of each. Core and remove some of the pulp to have room for the stuffing. Chop the pulp for the filling and save the hat.

4. To make the filling, sauté the diced onion, celery, and carrot in 2 tablespoons of butter until soft and just golden. Add the chopped quince and cook until softened. Add the ground lamb and brown. Add the split peas, thyme, fennel seeds, and cinnamon and 1 cup of stock. Season to taste with salt and pepper. Cook over low heat 5 to 10 minutes, then fold in the currants and bread crumbs. Transfer to a bowl to cool.

5. Preheat the oven to 350°F.

6. Season the inside cavity of the quinces with salt and pepper, then stuff with the sausage mixture and arrange to fit snugly in a buttered ovenproof baking dish.

7. Boil 1 cup of stock with the apple cider, honey, 3 tablespoons of butter, vinegar, saffron, and allspice, then pour a little of the mixture over each quince. Top each with a nugget of butter and replace its hat, poking the center with a clove to resemble a stem. Sprinkle with salt and pepper. Pour the remaining cider mixture around the quinces to come a quarter of the way up the sides of the fruit. Cover the dish and bake for 2 hours. If after the first hour there is no more liquid in the baking dish, add a little more cider.

8. Remove the cover, spoon the cooking juices over the fruit to moisten, and cook an additional 15 minutes, or until golden and tender but not mushy.

9. Serve on its own or with sautéed greens, rice, or polenta.

Cardamom Honey Madeleines

....

Chances are, if I walk into a bakery in France with the intention of buying a brioche or a coffee éclair, I'll walk out with a madeleine instead. When I was a student, I splurged once in a while and bought one—so simple and perfectly contained in its golden shell—to bring home to dunk in my tea. I learned to make each one last.

The cardamom is optional in this recipe. It is fun to experiment with varieties of honey found at your local farmers' market. Wildflower, buckwheat, lavender—each lends a distinct flavor to this true classic, and you can make several different batches for a tea party.

Makes 1 dozen 3-inch madeleines

4 ounces (1 stick) unsalted butter (2 tablespoons for the mold
    and 6 tablespoons for brown butter)
1 tablespoon honey
¼ teaspoon fresh-ground cardamom seeds
2 large eggs
1 tablespoon dark brown sugar
5 tablespoons granulated sugar
¼ teaspoon salt
¾ cup flour, plus 1 tablespoon for dusting the mold
1 teaspoon baking powder

1. Brush the insides of the madeleine mold with 2 tablespoons of softened butter, making sure to grease the indentations. Dust lightly with flour and tap the excess out.

2. In a saucepan, melt the remaining butter over medium heat. The butter will go through several stages, from foamy white to a golden liquid with big bubbles. When the butter begins to brown and gives off a nutty scent (after 4 to 5 minutes), transfer to a bowl to stop cooking and leave to cool. Stir the honey and cardamom into the butter.

3. In the bowl of an electric mixer with the whisk attachment, combine the eggs, sugars, and salt until the mixture thickens and becomes light in color.

4. Sift together the flour and baking powder. Fold the dry ingredients into the eggs alternately with the brown butter and honey, being careful not to overwork the mixture.

5. Cover the batter with plastic wrap and refrigerate for 2 hours. A cold batter makes the madeleines rise and form a beautiful dome.

6. Preheat the oven to 375°F.

7. Spoon the batter into the prepared molds, filling them almost to the top.

8. Bake for 10 to 12 minutes, until light golden and springy to the touch. Remove from the oven and invert the tray onto a wire

rack while the madeleines are still hot. If necessary, use the tip of a sharp knife to loosen them from the mold.

9. Serve the madeleines just as they are, barely cooled or at room temperature. When completely cool, they may be stored for several days in an airtight container.

Chapter 13

....

MY MOTHER WAS not at her grandson's third birthday party at the farm with the pony rides, where he learned to count to three in Farsi, holding up three plump fingers to my face to answer, *Seh!* to the question, *Sugar, how old are you today?* My sister gave me a box of little boys' ties she had found while cleaning out my mother's closet—an anguished task she undertook while I tackled the kitchen cabinets. My mother had intended the ties to be worn by her grandson to his first symphony, his first recital, his first wedding party; that these milestones will come and go without her is unthinkable. We simply lack her joie de vivre, her appetite for celebration, her easy way of gathering people together. Our attempts at celebration are maladroit: Christmas comes and I squeeze my son into the red sweater she knit for him with Santa smoking a pipe, we vow to make the longest paper chain ever, we make gingerbread houses and string lights. Noruz comes in March and I bungle through the traditional preparations, setting the *haftsin,* with its seven symbolic dishes. I color eggs with my son, we buy goldfish and he names them, drawing from the funny Farsi words he has learned: Haji, Chi Chi, FerFerry, Bah Bah, and so on. I layer filo dough with ground pistachios and cardamom to make baklava. The bank teller saves me rolls of shiny dollar coins to give to children. But all of this, all of it, falls short of her exuberance.

In a house that smelled of cardamom tea and roses, she insisted on the rituals of feeding her family and friends. Her home always welcomed guests; the *sofreh,* her tablecloth, was never folded away. Someone's coming for a cup of tea was a celebration; fruit would be washed and arranged in a bowl, sponge cakes and cream puffs lined up on doilies, dainty plates and cloth napkins stacked on a tray. This was not fussy, but rather matter-of-fact and generous: *Nonsense, you're staying for dinner!* Nothing was more vital than this, this gathering with you at her table. You heard her big, open laugh long after you left her house, and you were never gone for long because you missed being loved like that.

My mother would have chosen a different good-bye. She liked to do things properly. Never leaving a room untidy, she rinsed her teacup and folded away her place mat before leaving for her morning walk. But she didn't come home from that last walk. That her death was so brutal, so untidy, is at odds with the elegant person she was.

I've heard people use the word *compass* when they talk

about their mothers. But I wonder if that's accurate when I consider using it in describing how imperfect my world is without her. Instruments like a compass, ruler, or scale, essential as they are, are not my everyday tools. I look for her because she encompassed my day-to-day life. She is gone, and that she is gone is my first thought every morning, and it is there all day, in my kitchen, in my car, when I bring in the groceries, when I make dinner, when I refill the bird feeder and pick lemons from my tree. I don't mean that I am lost, but that I'm looking for her in the arc of my day, wondering what she would have to say about that driver who cut me off, or whether it's too early to plant bulbs, or how to tend an African violet. Strange how I don't miss her the way I used to. I don't stand bereft in my bedroom unable to remember what it is I had to do. I imagine we're swimming a parallel course, not meeting, but lifting an arm to wave, then paddling back to move forward.

When feelings well up from the past, a longing for a voice, a place, I reach for the manila envelope that holds her recipes. If I knew how to sew, perhaps I'd look through her sewing basket for the measuring tape, the velvet pincushion I bought her in Chinatown one Christmas, the buttons in the cookie tin. But I'm a cook, so I look at her recipes. I may or may not make the noodle casserole, but this time the rice pudding calls to me, and once I pour milk and sugar in the saucepan and stir in the rice, the feeling whittles away. When I go for a walk, I look at the world with her wonder—pulling thyme that pushes through a crack in the sidewalk, pocketing an interesting rock for my son, nudging the adventurous earthworm back to soil—and when I do, I am not ever without her.

Like a swimmer going forward by moving water back, I will never stop reaching into the past to trace the currents that converged here. In the shadows, I see larger-than-life images of my parents and wonder how I will measure up against their courage, their tenacity, their bigheartedness. I don't want to be a mere keeper of static memories, held captive by sorrow for what was lost; I mean to draw inspiration from their lives. Each time I look back, I pull on a thread and unravel a story I can share with my family, one that is fluid, with familiar characters, one that illuminates our nights together, allowing them to picture my father's hospital, the cranky donkey, the Caspian shore. I will surely repeat myself and I may not succeed each time in conjuring a compelling past, but perhaps I'll engage them through the prism of food.

Gazing back at my family's experience, it is with an eye to the immense gap between life as it ought to be and life as it actually is: what my parents had hoped to accomplish for their country, and their reversal of allegiance; what I would have become in Iran, and what became of me in America. My mother worked hard to bridge that gap, to make our home here. And in building that bridge, she made certain that I knew where I had come from, what I had left behind, and what I would find on the other side.

Rice Pudding

Sometimes rice pudding is the only thing that cures the blues. I remember being scolded once by my grandfather for reaching into one of his pigeons' cages for a tiny egg that I let slip from my hand. The louder he yelled, the noisier the pigeons cooed, and I was trapped by their erratic flutter around my ankles. I took refuge in my grandmother's kitchen, where I sat on a step stool and cried and she soothed me with a bowl of rice pudding scented with rose water.

Serves 6

2¼ cups whole milk
½ vanilla bean or 1 teaspoon vanilla extract
⅓ cup arborio rice
2½ tablespoons sugar
¼ cup rose water
1 cup heavy cream

1. Pour the milk into a medium saucepan. Split the vanilla bean, scrape out the seeds from the pod with the tip of a sharp knife, and add the seeds to the milk. Bring to a simmer.

2. Stir in the rice and simmer for 25 minutes, stirring occasionally, until it is the consistency of oatmeal. Stir in the sugar and cook for 5 more minutes.

3. Transfer the pudding to a bowl, and when it has cooled, fold in the rose water, then chill.

4. Whip the cream to soft peaks and gently fold into the rice for a creamy texture.

5. Serve in glass bowls with a dollop of jam, or a sprinkling of pistachio brittle (see following recipe), or all by itself.

Pistachio Brittle

. . . .

½ tablespoon butter for greasing the pan
1 cup peeled, lightly toasted pistachios
A pinch of salt
¾ cup sugar

1. Butter a cookie sheet.

2. Toss the pistachios in a bowl with a pinch of salt.

3. Place the sugar in a medium saucepan over high heat. As
   the sugar begins to caramelize, gently swirl the pan without
   stirring. Once it has reached a rich caramel brown, remove
   from the heat and fold in the pistachios with a wooden spoon.
   Spread onto the greased cookie sheet and cool.

4. Break into small pieces and store in an airtight container.

Chapter 14

ONE SUMMER AFTERNOON, I sat in my mother's kitchen with a notebook and pencil, sipping a Coke with lemon she had made for me. I watched as she moved from sink to stove, fetching a colander to strain the rice, melting a pad of butter in her *dig,* a large pot for cooking rice, steam rising from the sink and dampening her face, and all the while she was singing instructions: *Soak it, boil it, strain it, and don't forget the salt!* Rice was the first dish I learned to cook. I was eight. I say that as though I learned on my first try, when in fact it was one of the lessons I had to learn over and over again.

Almost forty years later, I find this scene repeating itself, only now my son sits watching me in the kitchen. He doesn't take notes yet, but he asks a lot of questions and he listens. And each time I recite a recipe, I'm unpacking another box, pulling open another drawer. The recipe doesn't tell him how to cook something; it tells a story that began on a school yard, in a garden, at the seaside, on a balcony, and how it smelled of jasmine that day, how it was so hot the butter melted right off the counter, how my grandfather yelled at me for filling the ice trays with hot water: *Do you know how hard that bloody refrigerator has to work to make ice?* How my mother sliced melons but let me scoop mine with a spoon, and how she shook the mulberry tree while I danced underneath, holding my skirt up to catch the falling berries:

How old were you, Maman?
I was seven.
Same age as me.
Yes.
Why did your grandpa yell at you?
It was so hot and he couldn't stand foolishness.
Did you cry?
No. We were used to him hollering.
Did you eat the "mallberries" out of your skirt?
As many as I could fit in my mouth.
Who do you miss more, your mom or your dad?
I miss my mom so much. We laughed a lot together.
I make you laugh, too, Maman.
Yes. Yes, you do.
Can she hear us laughing?

My son is greedy to hear again and again the stories I'm unpacking, but I know one day he will say: *You've told me this story a hundred times already!* By then, he will know what was lost and what was found, and how he, like the recipe, is a little bit of this and a sprinkling of that, how his humor is his grandmother's and his hands are his father's. In the meantime, he will have learned to make a perfect poached egg, corn bread, a pot of rice.

Last night we read the story *Stone Soup,* and he laughed when I told him about Ahmed Agha, the hospital chef my sisters sabotaged by putting pebbles in his food. I told him that the soldiers in the folktale, who stumble into town, tired and hungry, are not unlike his grandparents, who came to America with nothing but a willingness. They won over the villagers, taught them to make soup with ingredients they said they didn't have, and brought them to the table to break bread. And all the while they cooked as if they knew a pleasant secret: the desire for food, security, and love is a shared thing. My mother began on the premise that we were all hungry and if we could just sit at the table together, and the soup was hot, and the bread came from the oven, we would know that we had not tasted anything that good in a long time. If she asked a neighbor for a recipe, she was just stopping to ask for directions. When she taught herself to make apple pie, she cubed the apples and cooked them slowly with sugar, clove, and cinnamon until they caramelized, and *then* she filled her pie crust. All those hundreds of casserole and corn bread recipes weren't translated word for word. They simply opened a door and invited you in, they told you a Pilgrim story, or a love story, or suggested a longing for sweet or savory. With each recipe, she sampled a slice of America; she solved a riddle, inching closer to belonging and pulling us along, easing our way home, here in this kitchen.

I SPREAD NEWSPAPER on the floor and give my son a pile of walnuts to crack. He likes them with feta and mint leaves wrapped in large squares of lavash bread in his lunch box. He smooths the paper with the palms of his hands and sits cross-legged, gripping my mother's ancient nutcracker in his little fist and squeezing his eyes shut with the effort. The rest of the house is dark, but the kitchen glows, and the light from the ceiling falls on one side of his face when he looks up at me to check if we have enough, and I swear that a wise old man lives behind those bright eyes, because he understands so much more than I do.

It's still early, too early to go to school. And in the long stretch of these quiet mornings together—only his voice and mine, and the gurgle of the coffee machine, and his spoon tapping against a pale blue cup while I stir cocoa on the stove—I know I'm finally home. I brought in a stool so he could climb up, knees first, to see his egg come to a boil. Bare legs dangle to and fro, and with the first bubbles, he counts to sixty twice for soft-boiled while I take out plates from the cupboard above the counter.

He fills this kitchen with warmth, so that even after I've walked him to school, come home and washed the breakfast plates, stacked them in the cupboard, wiped the stove and gathered the walnut shells, and laid my mother's nutcracker in the middle drawer next to her spoon, I still feel his warmth.

My Mother's Apple Pie

Not too long ago, I was reading a book called Each Peach Pear
Plum, *by Janet and Allan Ahlberg. It is a lovely "I spy" book, where
favorite nursery characters hide in the pictures and the rhyme pro-
vides the clues to their whereabouts. In a delightful ending, Jack and
Jill, the Three Bears, Tom Thumb, and a host of others come out
of their hiding places to eat plum pie. It was like seeing old friends
at a reunion, my son pointing in recognition as each one emerged:*
Oh, look, there's Old Mother Hubbard! *The illustration of that
pie, with its golden dome in the center of a blue checkered picnic
blanket, was evocative of a picture book my mother read to me when
I was four or five. What I remember from that story is the drawing
of an apple pie on a table set with cups and saucers, and my instant
longing for it. I asked her if she could make one that looked just like
that. I'll try, she said.*

*My mother taught herself to make apple pie. She didn't have a
taste for the starchy, raw filling in soggy bottomed pies, so she applied her baking knowledge and made this delicious version of the
American classic. It is the best I have ever tasted.*

Serves 8

Pastry for a double-crust pie (see following recipe)
12 to 15 Golden Delicious, Granny Smith, or Pippin apples
5 tablespoons butter
3 cups sugar, plus 1 tablespoon

2 teaspoons cinnamon

1 egg yolk

1 tablespoon milk

1. Peel and core the apples, then dice into about ¼-inch pieces. In a large skillet, melt 3 tablespoons of butter and sauté the apples over medium-high heat for about 5 minutes. If necessary, cook them in 2 batches so as not to crowd them in your pan. Add the sugar and cinnamon and stir with a wooden spoon to distribute the sugar evenly. Don't worry about the liquid that will be released once the sugar begins to melt. Continue stirring often so that the apples on the bottom won't burn. Cook the apples until they have caramelized but are not mushy, about 20 to 25 minutes.

2. Spread the apples on a baking sheet to cool completely.

3. To assemble the pie, divide the dough into 2 unequal halves, the larger half for the bottom crust and the smaller for the top.

4. Roll the larger half on a lightly floured surface until it is about ⅛ inch thick and large enough to fit your pie dish with about 1 inch extra to overlap the edges. Chill while you roll out the remainder of the dough.

5. On a lightly floured surface, roll out the smaller half of the dough until it is about ⅛ inch thick and large enough to top the pie.

6. Fill the pie shell with the cooled, sautéed apples, shaped into a pyramid, and dot with the remaining 2 tablespoons of butter. Lay the top crust over the apples and press gently to form. With your thumb and fingertips, pinch the bottom and top crust together to seal, trimming the extra dough with a knife.

7. Poke a hole in the center with the tip of a knife and cut 2 or 3 slits around the hole to allow steam to escape. Refrigerate for 30 minutes. It is possible to make this pie and freeze it to bake later, a particularly helpful technique during feverish holiday baking marathons.

8. Preheat the oven to 375°F.

9. Beat 1 egg yolk with 1 tablespoon of milk to brush the top of your pie. Sprinkle with a tablespoon of sugar. Place the pie on the middle shelf of the oven with a baking sheet below to catch the juices in case they drip. Bake 1 hour, until the top crust is golden brown.

Pie Pastry

Makes enough for 1 double-crust pie

8 ounces (2 sticks) chilled, unsalted butter
3½ cups flour
1 teaspoon salt
1 cup ice water

1. Cut the butter into ½-inch cubes and toss with the flour and salt. Crumble the butter into the flour by rubbing your thumbs and fingertips together until the mixture resembles cornmeal. Slowly add the water, ¼ cup at a time, until the mixture just comes together.

2. Gather the dough to form a smooth ball. Refrigerate for 1 hour.

3. If using a food processor or electric mixer, make the dough in the same order but be careful not to overmix. This dough keeps well for a few days in the refrigerator, and up to 1 month in the freezer.

Cherry Slushy

. . . .

When my son asked me to make him a slushy, his request hearkened back to a story I had once told him about snow days in Iran. We were cuddled up reading Ezra Jack Keats's The Snowy Day, *when I remembered waking up to a blanket of snow outside my window and running to the kitchen to tune in to the station that announced school closures. If we heard the name of our school, we screamed in unison, then spent the morning eating breakfast in our pajamas before bundling up to go play. We returned hours later, shivering and soaked through to our underwear. For an afternoon snack, my mother would look for a clean patch of snow to scoop into little bowls and pour sour cherry syrup on top.* They're going to get sick! *my father would protest, but nothing can stop a child from putting snow in her mouth and tasting it to understand the miracle of it.*

The first time we took my son to see snow, I watched him licking a snowball and stopped myself as I was about to take it away from him. At home in California, I had to improvise to make him some-thing that resembled what my mother had made, and it is in fact a Persian granita made with shredded rice noodles.

Serves 6

3 cups sugar

1¼ cups water

2 lemons, juice and zest

3 tablespoons rose water

5 ounces thin rice noodles, broken up

½ cup cherry preserves in syrup

1 lime

1. Place sugar, water, lemon juice, and zest in a medium saucepan. Stir and bring to a boil. Remove from heat and cool. Stir in the rose water.

2. Bring a pot of water to a boil. Remove from heat. Immerse the rice noodles in hot water and let stand for 8 to 10 minutes, stirring occasionally. Soak until the noodles are soft but firm. Strain, rinse with cold water, and set aside.

3. Pour the sugar syrup into a 12 × 8-inch Pyrex dish, or any equivalent glass or porcelain dish. Spread the rice noodles evenly in the syrup and place in the freezer. Every hour or so, remove from the freezer and stir the mixture up delicately with the tines of a fork, breaking up the ice crystals that form around the edge of the dish to avoid freezing it into a solid block.

4. Freeze up to 8 hours. It is best served the day it is made. To serve, shave the slushy into chilled bowls and swirl with cherry preserves and a generous squeeze of lime.

Special Thanks

. . . .

THIS BOOK WOULD not have been written without the unwavering belief and encouragement of my husband, Mitchell Johnson, the sensitive insight and generous guidance of my editor, Andra Miller, and the keen instincts of my agent, Adam Chromy, who embraced and championed this project. Their confidence urged me forward. I cannot thank them enough.

My love and thanks to my sisters, Shabnam Anderson and Sherry Bijan, who were my first teachers and shared many of these memories, and to my brilliant nieces, Sophia and Helene, for their culinary enthusiasm and shared meals.

My immense gratitude to all the great chefs in my life who set the bar very high, and everyone I had the privilege to work with at L'Amie Donia. Warm thanks to Karla Ebrahimi and Jean Mellott for their patient testing and feedback on my recipes, and to the extraordinary team at Algonquin for their support; in particular I am grateful to David Matt, Elisabeth Scharlatt, Anne Winslow, Brunson Hoole, Rachel Careau,

Sarah Rose Nordgren, Kelly Bowen, Megan Fishmann, Michael Taeckens, Craig Popelars, and Ina Stern.

You live inside your parents' lives until, one day, they live inside yours. I'm thankful to the memory of my mother and father, who continue to be my unerring guides. I owe them everything.

And above all, I must thank my beloved son, whose appetite for stories and food lights up our meals and makes us laugh out loud everyday. This book is for you.